Theology, Death and Dying

Theology, Death and Dying

RAY S. ANDERSON

© Ray S. Anderson 1986

First published 1986

Basil Blackwell Ltd
108 Cowley Road, Oxford OX4 1JF, UK

Basil Blackwell Inc.
432 Park Avenue South, Suite 1503,
New York, NY 10016, USA

British Library Cataloguing in Publication Data
Anderson, Ray S.
 Theology, death and dying.
 1. Death — Religious aspects —
 Christianity
 I. Title
 248.4   BT825

 ISBN 0–631–14846–9
 ISBN 1-881266-01-X Pbk

Library of Congress Cataloging in Publication Data
Anderson, Ray Sherman
 Theology, death, and dying.

 Bibliography: p.
 Includes index.
 1. Death — Religious aspects — Christianity.
I. Title.
BT825.A49 1986   236'.1   85–30806
ISBN 0–631–14846–9
ISBN 1-881266-01-X (pbk.)

Typeset by Oxford Publishing Services
Printed in Great Britain by Billing and Sons Ltd, Worcester

Contents

Preface

On a lazy summer Sunday afternoon, without apparent premeditation, my parents would suddenly announce a trip to the local rural cemetery for the purpose of tending some family grave sites. Of course we children were included. It was not a long trip, for the cemetery adjoined the farm on which we lived on the flat prairie-land of middle America.

The simple rituals of pulling some weeds, clipping some grass and digging up the soil around a straggling, flowering plant were quickly accomplished, and served only as a pretext for the visit, as it usually turned out.

Trailing behind, as my parents wandered from grave site to grave site, I heard the litany of their commentary on the dead. 'Here's where the Torstensons are buried. Wasn't she a Carlson girl who came over with her parents from the old country, and didn't they homestead the quarter section next to the old Anderson farm where I was born?', my father would ask.

And so it went. These were not questions, but statements. Statements about a community in which the boundary between the living and the dead lost its sharp edge of terror. This was a mystery which was part of the fabric of life. What this small boy experienced was the easy familiarity with which this uncanny boundary was traversed. But even more, what was experienced was the wordless testimony that this excursion was an event in which their faith was enacted. Implicit in this patriarchal pageantry was a statement about what they believed; and death was not alien to this belief system.

What did my father think about when he tended the grave sites and contemplated the plot where he himself would one day be buried? Did he have anxiety? Did he fear that death would annihilate all of the meaning of his life to that point? Did he have the feeling that he was sinking into an oblivion which would be a place of peace and rest from self conscious worry and fretful toil? Or did he have in his mind a hope for continuing self conscious life beyond the grave, and if so, how did he envision this?

What did he think when he passed the small grave marker and commented, 'Yes, and here is the two year old Peterson boy; he was kicked in the head by a cow and died that very night'? Had he ever questioned the fairness of that? Had he ever questioned God about that?

I don't know. He never said. Death and God were the two things that were never openly questioned. Perhaps the question and the answer had become so fused that faith was as simple as a Sunday afternoon walk in the cemetery and planting a straight row of corn.

The final stop, before getting into the car, was always a quiet moment spent tidying a green plot with no graves yet dug, marked only with the single headstone – ANDERSON. This plot has now been filled, of course. And not too far away there is another plot which has been purchased which not only signals my own anticipation of joining this 'processional', but which is also a statement about what I believe, about life and about death. I am not, because of distance, granted the privilege of being the 'caretaker' of my own place of burial; nor have my children ever visited the site.

What will they believe about death? And what are the resources out of which they will create that belief? Obviously they are not the same as mine; and yet, from childhood on, we search for an answer to the phenomenon of death and, one way or another, come to think about our own death.

Children ask questions about death out of curiosity. Their innocence permits them this luxury. They have not yet learned that the most holy and the most intimate do not yield their secrets to the curious. Whether the terror of death is the approach of the holy, we are not sure. But we do know by now that death is far too intimate for us to ply questions merely out of curiosity.

To write a book about death is to stare straight into the dark tunnel towards which life inexorably leads. Only the innocent or the clever would think otherwise: I am neither.

At best, this attempt is a sideways glance at the subject of death. This is as it should be, for it is an attempt to state a theology of death from a Christian perspective. Death can never be the centre of focus in a Christian perspective. Christian theology is a theology of life – of creation, not corruption; of meaning, not despair; of light, not darkness.

The book, as a consequence, has a bias. It is written from a perspective that has two points of reference. The first is that of a Christian theology which begins out of the centre of God's revelation in Jesus Christ. Thus, what is presented here is not a general theology of death, but a *Christian* theology of death. The perspective is Christian in the sense that Christ is the one who speaks to us from the other side of death. While other perspectives and other theologies of death are recognized in the discussion, there is no attempt to cover all of the wide-ranging views of death, either from a historical perspective or in our contemporary world.

The focus of the book is thus closely controlled by a perspective of 'faith seeking understanding' (*fides quaerens intellectum*). My purpose is to examine death from within the circle of faith in Jesus Christ as the Lord of life, who has overcome death.

There is a second perspective, which contributes to the bias of the book. I confess to an interest in death which goes beyond academic and scholarly objectivity. My assumption is that the reader is not unacquainted with the feeling. A good theology is also a deeply felt and lived one. A theology of death is, to some extent at least, a testimony to what one believes and by what one lives, as well as careful reflection upon revealed truth.

The reader is asked to allow the occasional personal references which I have included. These are not meant to provide anecdotal relief, but are windows through which we can look at death with the eyes of Christian faith.

Kierkegaard, in his *Concluding Unscientific Postscript*, once wrote that one who speaks of death ought to give an ethical expression for the significance of death, a religious expression for victory over death, a resolving word to explain its mystery, and a binding word by which the individual defends himself.

I should be happy to feel that I have made some attempt in this regard.

Ray S. Anderson

CHAPTER 1

The Question of Death and the Christian Answer

Death is an event that requires explanation. Every human society has recognized the importance of orientating its members to the phenomenon of death, the process of dying and death's aftermath. So powerful is the event of death and its demand for interpretation that it may well have been one of the first causes of religion and philosophy in primitive people. To confront human mortality is a basic human need. Any theology that ignored death would be inadequate, and any philosophy of life that avoided providing an answer to death, superficial.

The Christian faith tradition, building on the foundations of ancient Israel's belief in God as the creator and sustainer of life, answers the question of death through its testimony to the death and resurrection of Jesus Christ. There are many theologies of death, even as there are many philosophies of death. While many of these will be noted in this book, the attempt will be to provide an answer to the question of death from the perspective of Christian theology.

Here too one must say that there is no single Christian theology of death upon which all would agree, even as there are a range of philosophical questions and opinions within a Christian theology of death. While this book will attempt to present various perspectives on death from within this broad Christian tradition, as well as take note of other traditions and other theologies of death, its purpose is to explore the answer which one perspective in Christian theology might give to the question of death.

In this first chapter the foundations for our theological inquiry into the subject of death will be set squarely upon the

historical and traditional beliefs of Christian faith. This
foundation is rooted in the confession that Jesus of Nazareth
died, and was raised from the dead by the power of God, and
that his resurrection is the hope of Christians in the face of
their own death.

In saying this, I am not unmindful of the fact that I am
addressing a generation for whom the dogmas of Christian
belief are far from evident in the face of the almost self evident
and relentless onslaught of scientific materialism and secular
humanism. Many who adhere intellectually to the traditional
teachings of the Church are none the less anything but secure
in their faith – particularly when it comes to the issue of death
and dying.

And what of those who no longer have either intellectual or
existential roots in the Christian faith tradition? What of those
for whom the world has 'come of age,' as Dietrich Bonhoeffer
liked to put it? If God is no longer a 'working hypothesis', a
deus ex machina, a 'stop-gap' when confronted with a situation
which is life-threatening, then will talk of God be even less
meaningful than the reality of death? If God has 'died', so to
speak, as an existential partner, and if the world is now totally
'worldly', can there be any such thing as a theologian or
theology?

We must listen carefully when Ignace Lepp, both a priest
and a practising psychotherapist, tells us: 'I doubt that the
meditations of the mystics or the speculations of theologians on
death can be of much existential help to such people.'[1]

We listen thoughtfully when the theologian Helmut
Thielicke reminds us that behind the question of death as a
philosophical or theological issue is the existential question,
'Why me?' This question 'Why?', says Thielicke, 'remains an
open one. It remains also an open wound through which faith
in the gods threatens to bleed to death.'[2]

This question becomes a classic text in the anguished words
of Ivan Ilych, as Leo Tolstoi tells the story:

The syllogism he had learnt from Kiezewetter's logic: 'Caius is a
man, men are mortal, therefore Caius is mortal,' had always
seemed to him correct as applied to Caius, but certainly not as
applied to himself. That Caius – man in the abstract – was
mortal, was perfectly correct, but he was not Caius, not an

abstract man, but a creature quite, quite separate from all others... 'Caius really was mortal, and it was right for him to die; but for me, little Vanya, Ivan Ilych, with all my thoughts and emotions, it's altogether a different matter. It cannot be that I ought to die. That would be too terrible... It's impossible! But here it is. How is this? How is one to understand it?'[3]

How indeed is one to understand death?

It is useless to continue to put the question in such a form, as though death itself could provide the answer. 'Death is mute', Eberhard Jüngel tells us, 'And it renders us speechless. If we are to speak about death at all, then a word must come from 'beyond' death. Christian faith makes the claim that it has heard such a word.'[4] Death itself cannot provide us with the answer to death, for the dead and death are in the same category. No one who questions death has experienced it, because it lies beyond experience. And no one who has experienced death can be questioned about it!

If our task then is that of a theological inquiry into the event of death from a Christian perspective, we need to establish first of all how theology proceeds to deal with an issue such as death.

The word 'theology' may be troublesome for many. Too often, theology has been represented as an academic exercise which is largely speculative and irrelevant to real life. This concept of theology surely lies behind the complaint of Ignace Lepp cited earlier. Theological discourse has not always been praised as being edifying discourse. *Mea culpa!*

We can learn from Jesus himself how theological inquiry proceeds out of the encounter with God in the midst of life.

Jesus took up theological discourse in the midst of the crisis of faith. This means that he spoke of the reality of God as present tense reality and as the power to summon forth faith. Not only that, faith that was summoned forth had a direct bearing on the living of life, and in some cases certainly, was actually life-restoring.

To Jairus, a ruler of the synagogue, whose daughter was pronounced dead, Jesus said, 'Do not fear, only believe'. And proceeding to the house, Jesus raised her from the dead (Mark 2:35–43). To the paralytic who was carried to Jesus to be healed, he said, 'Your sins are forgiven'. A theological inquiry was conducted by Jesus on the spot when this was considered blasphemy. 'Why do you question thus in your hearts? Which is easier, to say to the paralytic, 'Your sins are forgiven,' or to say, 'Rise, take up your pallet and walk'? But that you may know that the Son of man has authority on earth to forgive sins. . . I say to you, rise, take up your pallet and go home.' (Mark 2:1–12).

In the context of the grief and despair following the death of Lazarus, Jesus not only shed his own tears, but brought a theological inquiry to the situation. 'I am the resurrection and the life;' said Jesus, 'he who believes in me, though he die, yet shall he live,. . . do you believe this?' And Martha answered, 'Yes, Lord; I believe that you are the Christ, the Son of God, he who is coming into the world' (John 11:17–44).

In the face of the apparent reality and finality of death, a reality of God was presented as the answer to which all questions are directed. This is what theology is all about. It is not speculation based upon questions which are ultimately unanswerable; it is questioning 'out of the answer', so to speak. Or, as T.F. Torrance has put it, it is 'questioning in Jesus Christ.'[5]

The validity of a theological inquiry with respect to the nature of death *is* of existential concern to those who experience a crisis of faith over the issues of death and dying. Jüngel warns us, 'If the answer to the question of death is not one which has the power to *set us free* (from uncertainty and from false ties), then this will simply mean that *faith* has no valid answer to this question.'[6]

Being 'set free' from death is the practical consequence of what we believe about death. This freedom is a favourite theme of the apostle Paul. Because the law convicts one of sin, and because sin is the 'sting of death,' the death of Jesus Christ sets us free from the law, from sin and from death (cf. Romans 6:5–23; 1 Corinthians 15:55–56). Even through the actual experience of physical death, one is freed from the power of death to destroy our life. This is held to be true because it is a consequence of the death and resurrection of Jesus Christ. This is what Christians believe to be the answer to death, and in holding this belief, they can feel set free from the power of death as a final event of meaninglessness and despair.

Richard Doss has suggested in his helpful essay, 'A Theological Style for Interpreting Death', that a theology of death becomes necessary if we really want to listen and respond to basic problems of human existence. 'In a sense', he writes,

> death calls the whole theological enterprise into question. Death forces us to examine the claim of Christian faith that in Jesus Christ a God of unconditional love offers new life and hope. . . And death also raises problems concerning the future, questions about a possible life after death and a final fulfillment of the goals and values experienced in this life. A theology of death must provide adequate response to these issues.[7]

Christian theology, therefore, is theological reflection upon the meaning of God's action in Jesus Christ. As an activity of faith in Christ, theological reflection is a form of questioning that faith undertakes precisely because there is confidence that God Himself is the answer to the need for assurance that human life will survive death.

In addition to faith *in Christ*, there is a second dimension to faith; this might be called a faith *from Christ*, as John Hick once put it.[8] Faith from Christ consists of the formulations which theological reflection offers as responses to contemporary issues in light of God's answer in Jesus Christ. One example of such theological reflection is the contemporary question of death and dying. This is what we mean by theological inquiry. It is a dynamic task, and one which must be done by every generation in light of new issues and challenges to faith *in* Christ.

The specific nature of the Christian claim appears to be that the death of Jesus Christ is the only human death which has become the answer to the enigma and mystery of all human deaths. This death is not just 'one among many', any more than the birth of Jesus was 'one among many'. The death which entered into the world through the first Adam, says Helmut Thielicke, is not the prototype of human death. Rather, the death of Jesus as the second Adam is the prototype for the death of every human person.[9] Through incarnation and crucifixion, the eternal God has made our death His by taking our humanity as His own form of being. Therefore, He also made His death ours, and His resurrection from the dead is the answer to our questions about death. This is the foundation for a Christian answer to the question of death.

The need for assurance and certainty in light of the challenge of death to human life is global in scope and culturally informed. The questions which faith asks, therefore, are not restricted to any one culture, or to any one time and place. The specific nature of a Christian inquiry, however, which begins with the answer as given by God in Jesus Christ, is thereby restricted methodologically to the gospel of Christ as the incarnate, crucified, and resurrected Son of God. This is what makes this theological inquiry into the nature of death a Christian theology of death.

From this foundation of a Christian answer to the question of death, we can now survey briefly some alternative answers, both from a theological and philosophical perspective.

A theology of death within contemporary Judaism, like that arising within the Christian tradition, will build upon foundations that are unique to the beginnings of Israel as a historical community, set within the temporal bounds of a created world. Death is a boundary to the historical existence of the Jew as well as a dividing line between the human and the divine. For the Jew, death comes from the hand of God, and has no power of its own. There is a relative indifference in the Old Testament scriptures to the length of life. The fact that Adam lived '930 years; and he died,' suggests nothing more than the fact that Adam satisfied his commitment to history, *and then he died* (Genesis 5:5).

The uniqueness of the biblical Jew, as one author has put it, is that 'when the Jews looked at death they saw life; and when they looked at life they saw God.'[10] Death does not have an arbitrary power to break continuity of life, because life is related to the continuity of God's purpose in history. It is precisely for this reason that the holocaust is of such consequence for the modern Jew. The horror of the holocaust is not alone the fact that over 6,000,000 Jews died, but that this event was a deliberate attempt to annihilate the history of the Jewish people on earth. If God is understood to be the guarantor of their history, and if their history comes to an end, then this means that death has triumphed over life.

Death is a threat when it has the power to effect a discontinuity which robs life of meaning. The Jew's unique understanding of the meaning of death lies with the affirmation that death marks an absolute end of personal existence on earth. Continuity does not consist, therefore, in a theory of personal immortality which extends the individual's life beyond death, but instead in the assurance of a future in which there is continuing conversation and relation between God and His people.

When the apostle Paul considers the possibility that God has rejected His people, he reacts strongly: 'By no means. . . God has not rejected his people whom he foreknew. . . so all Israel will be saved' (Romans 11:1,2,26). Paul does not appear to hold that the death of individual Jews breaks the continuity of the promise, 'all Israel shall be saved'. This can explain to us why the doctrine of personal immortality and the survival of the person after death is not a major part of a Jewish theology of death.

When we look at the theology of death represented in a religion such as Hinduism, we find a quite different concept of death. For the Hindu, continuity of life is not connected with concrete personal, historical existence as such, but rather in the concept of *being* which is contrasted with both life and death. Life and death are a form of *existence*, which is not real in the sense that being is real. Because life has a beginning, and has come into existence, it is not real. Life as existence, along with its pleasures and pain, is not real. Therefore, death is not the loss of being as such, but merely the end of the illusion of life as existence in time. 'That which is non-existent can never come into being', says the *Bhagavad-Gita*, 'and that which is can never cease to be. Those who have known the inmost Reality know also the nature of *is* and *is not*.'[11]

While the concepts that comprise the core of the Hindu religion are complex and subtle, it is clear that the cycle of life and death is part of the illusion that clings to all existence. What is real, what has continuity, is *being* – the Atman. Even selfhood as personal existence is an illusion, and only the Atman present in the illusion of life and death is real. Thus, death is not a power which threatens the real, for being cannot begin to exist nor can it cease to exist.

For the Buddhist, on the other hand, the self exists as a sheer moment in history, of becoming in history. History itself has no meaning apart from what one becomes in the moment of history. The stream of history goes nowhere; history does not take us somewhere, but constitutes the 'banks' which channel the stream of selfhood as sheer illumination or enlightenment. Life and death as a process of time and history are fictions which prod the self to discover the liberation of the self from reflection and feeling alike.

Death is not an enemy in Buddhist theology; instead it is the goad which produces a liberation from the cravings and sensations of life. The craving for life as well as the fear of death are both fictions, and stand as barriers to the unmediated joy of sheer identity with all that is. In this way, death is not a problem to be overcome for the sake of the continuity of personal identity. Rather, identity is itself a freedom from causality and connectedness which inhere in the life/death continuum.[12]

When we look back at the concept of death in ancient Greek philosophy, we see a quite different answer to the question of death. Here there is a concern for immortality as a specific object of philosophical reality. Whereas the Jew finds continuity in the purpose of history as a dialogue with God, the Hindu in the Atman as the reality of being, and the Buddhist in the contentless moment of not-knowing, the Greek philosopher seeks continuity in knowledge as the eternal reality.

Socrates, as Plato records his conversations, is not the least perturbed over the fact of his own approaching demise from earthly existence. To live is to take up timeless residence in 'true knowledge'. What we call life, with its changing forms and unstable realities, is really like a stage upon which the timeless conversation with true knowledge takes place. When the curtain closes on the final act (death), the real drama continues unhindered by the unsubstantial forms of bodily and earthly existence. Continuity is achieved through the soul's own immortal relation to the eternal truths. Death has been dissolved of its power to destroy the self; because all of life itself in its bodily form is only of passing significance, death too is viewed only as a passing away of that which is unnecessary to the true personality of the soul.[13]

What appears to be a common assumption between the Hindu, Buddhist and Greek concept of death is a fundamental dualism with regard to the reality of the 'otherworldly' and the unreality of this present temporal existence. While there are important philosophical differences between them, these are representative of all dualistic views of reality in which the historical and temporal are not taken seriously as real expressions of personal identity. In removing from death the power of effecting a discontinuity in the reality of the self, these attempts to explain death undermine the reality of life as defined in terms of temporal and historical existence.

The Jewish theology of death, on the other hand, opposes such a dualism by placing both life and death within the created boundedness of historical and temporal existence. Continuity is achieved through an identification of the individual person with the corporate person in the form of the survival of the ethnic community as a people with whom God remains in dialogue. The individual Israelite achieves immortality in the 'all Israel shall be saved'.

A Christian theology of death stands in stark contrast to the dualism of the Greek, Hindu and Buddhist theology of life and death. There is a closer affinity between the Christian and Jewish perspective on death, as one might suspect. Both take seriously the reality of temporal, historical existence as the embodiment of personal being. Both view the human self as created and subject to the conditions of mortal existence. Both seek continuity of personal existence through a relationship to God in both life and death.

There remains, however, a fundamental difference as well between the Christian and Jewish views of death. This difference can be seen in the fundamental rejection of the Christian claim that the historical person, Jesus of Nazareth is the Messiah and that his life, death and resurrection is the basis for continuity of existence through death for all persons, both Jew and Gentile. This distinctively Pauline view of Jesus Christ appeared to become determinative for the New Testament's theology of death. It is the one man, Jesus Christ, argues Paul, who carries the continuity of all men from Adam onwards through death into eternal life. If death came through the first man (Adam), and death reigned as a result of sin in all men, so, says Paul, in the second man (Jesus Christ), has death been destroyed and eternal life granted to all men (Romans 5:18–21).

We have been looking at some representative concepts of death as expressed in traditional religious and philosophical views. These have in common what might be called a theological assumption that there is a purpose or meaning that can be discerned out of some transcendent quality or reality of life, often described in terms of a divine being or reality.

There is also a more modern attempt to explain death in terms that avoid any reference to a transcendent being or reality beyond death. In these attempts, death itself is defined as a limiting concept which can be seen to be a positive factor in giving life meaning and reality.

Death, as a limiting concept, can make affirmative contributions to life, insists John Macquarrie. Life without end would be an intolerable experience. Death places life within a definite framework of time, enabling the individual to measure the events of life with utmost seriousness. Death can even 'redeem a thitherto unworthy or mediocre life,' he asserts, and 'this can be argued without any appeal whatever to the possibility of life beyond death'.[14]

The same theme can be found in many forms of contemporary existential philosophy. Against the silence of death, existence continues to argue its case as having ultimate meaning without reference to a transcendent reality beyond death. Following the lead of Heidegger, the existentialist philosopher leans on 'being' as a pole on which he can vault over 'non-being'. Individual being (*Dasein*) is a 'being-toward-death' argued Heidegger,[15] and as such it is the ontological possibility of authentic existence precisely in this orientation towards death.

The current interest in death, suggests Peter Koestenbaum, originated with the existential philosophers, and has now been taken over by the existential psychologists. Koestenbaum himself, a philosopher by trade, urges us to consider death as a 'hermeneutical event' which defines the individual as both concrete and universal. Death, in his view, is thus necessary to give existential meaning to life.[16] John Hick suggests that without the boundary of death we would not even be human persons, with love, hate, hope and fear as part of our personal being.[17]

James Carse states his thesis even more boldly: 'Death, perceived as discontinuity, is not that which robs life of its meaning, but that which makes life's meaningfulness possible.'[18]

Even the venerable Heidegger comes under criticism by his countryman, Arnold Metzger, for his lack of authentic

(Christian) despair, for the lack of yearning for the transcendence of the infinite. The Being that breaks through finiteness, for Heidegger, is eliminated. Instead, Metzger argues, we should see death as the horizon between the finite and infinite in such a way that 'the presence of eternity is inherent in every sensory present'. 'The dying moment endures forever', sings Metzger, 'The horizon of permanent duration is associated with the sensory content, i.e., with the reproduction that is linked to the dying moment.'[19]

One cannot help but wonder if these speculations are not in the honourable tradition of Plato, who was known to have said that philosophy is the rehearsal of death, and true philosophers make dying their profession.[20]

Let us return now to consider the central thesis for a Christian answer to the question of death. Death is not a limiting concept which gives meaning to life; rather, the meaning of death must be found in the meaning of the death of Jesus Christ. For Christians, what is believed about death cannot be based on some 'inner meaning' which death has for us as a philosophical concept. Death is no mere abstraction, nor can it be made meaningful as an abstract concept. There must be meaning to death precisely because there must be meaning to each individual's death. It is in the historical life and death of Jesus Christ that Christian theology finds its answer to the meaning of death.

As a Christian theologian, Jüngel points the way forward by suggesting that if we are to speak about death at all then there must be a word which comes to us from beyond death. It is the claim of Christian faith that it has heard this word. This word then comes to us in the midst of our life, not at the limiting horizon of death. Yes, it is true, as Jüngel says, '. . . man's life stands in a relationship with death'. However, he adds, 'Life is the source of information about death.'[21]

Christian theology, then, does not look for answers to come out of death, nor does it see its task as an attempt to draw forth hermeneutical implications for life out of death as a limitation and horizon of life. No, for Christian theology the answer comes to us in the middle of life, not at its boundary. The so-called frontier situations (Jaspers), or limiting situations (Tillich), are not where the answers are to be found, but in Jesus Christ, who meets us in the centre of life.

Dietrich Bonhoeffer was faithful to this tenet of Christian theology when he said that the revelation of God, or the borderline 'no longer passes through man as such, or can be drawn by him, but is Christ himself'.[22] Man's limit is in the middle of his existence, not on the edge, wrote Bonhoeffer: 'The limit which we look for on the edge is the limit of his condition, of his technology, of his possibilities. The limit in the middle is the limit of his reality, of his true existence.'[23] This theme takes a more Christological expression in Bonhoeffer's thought when he says: 'Here again, God is no stop-gap; he must be recognized at the centre of life, not when we are at the end of our resources; . . . in our activities, and not only in sin. The ground for this lies in the revelation of God in Jesus Christ.'[24]

Death cannot serve as the ultimate limiting concept in this view. God Himself is the limit, and Christian theology asserts the belief that God has revealed Himself in Jesus Christ. In the human person, Jesus of Nazareth, in his life, death and resurrection, we discover what death means for all humans.

The task of theology is to give appropriate expression to the answer which has come to us through Jesus Christ in contemporary terms. The theology of faith, says Helmut Thielicke, is a hermeneutic of the Easter event of the resurrection of Jesus from the dead, worked out through a critical anthropology.[25]

Jüngel too suggests that a theological anthropology has to be developed prior to a theology of death. This is for the sake of making a correction of the Greek dualist anthropology which has permeated Christian anthropology with a resulting depreciation of human life (and so human death) in favour of an unwarranted emphasis on concepts of immortality.[26]

While there is indeed an anthropological concern at the heart of the question about death – for it is human death that is the issue – the answer as to the nature and meaning of human life must preceue the question as to the nature and meaning of death. This is why our task is a theological one, because it inquires into the meaning of death for Jesus Christ as representative of all humanity.

This book is written, and is presumably being read, by those who are not actually facing death. We are thinking about death, we are questioning death, and we are apprehensive about death. We have awareness of death, even though we may not actually be at the point of death. Yet this may well be the point where faith becomes most uncertain and fearful. It may be true for us, as Pascal once said, 'Death when one does not think about it is more bearable than the thought of death when one is not in danger.'[27]

We are more aware of death today than we have ever been. But we are less familiar with the process of dying. 'Death has been a very badly kept secret,' says Michael Simpson.[28] There is denial of death, repression of death, and the professional separation of the dying from the living. Yet, we cannot escape from our fear of death.

This chapter has not attempted to define death itself. Instead, it has suggested that the answer to our questions about death is to be found in the life, death and resurrection of Jesus Christ. The task of a theology of death is to provide this answer in the context of contemporary thinking about death.

Before we can proceed further with our theological reflection on death, we need to make an assessment of the contemporary mind and its concerns and perspectives about death. Is death something which we prefer not to think about, or is it something which we think about but pretend not to see? This is what we will find out in the next chapter.

NOTES

1 *Death and Its Mysteries* (New York: Macmillan, 1968).
2 *Living With Death* (Grand Rapids: Eerdmans, 1983), p. 8.
3 L. Tolstoi, *The Death of Ivan Ilych* (New York: Health Sciences Publishing, 1973), pp. 43–44. In his important work, *Being and Time*, translated by John Macquarrie and Edward Robinson (New York: Harper and Row, 1962), Martin Heidegger acknowledges his own indebtedness to Tolstoi in a footnote: 'In his story, "The Death of Ivan Ilych", Leo Tolstoi has presented the phenomenon of the disruption and breakdown of having "someone die"' (p. 495). Walter Kaufmann goes so far as to say that Heidegger's thesis of the individual as 'being-toward-death' is, 'for the most part an unacknowledged commentary on *The Death of Ivan Ilyitch*': see 'Existentialism and Death,' in *The Meaning of Death*, edited by Herman Feifel (New York: McGraw-Hill, 1959), p. 45.
4 *Death: The Riddle and the Mystery*, (Philadelphia: Westminster Press, 1974), preface.
5 *Theology in Reconstruction* (Grand Rapids: Eerdmans, 1965).
6 *Death: The Riddle and the Mystery*, p. 27.
7 *The Last Enemy* (New York: Harper and Row, 1974), p. 19.
8 *Faith and Knowledge* (Ithaca, NY: Cornell University Press, 1966), p. 217.
9 *Living With Death*, p. 164.
10 James P. Carse, *Death and Existence: A Conceptual History of Human Mortality* (New York: John Wiley, 1980), p. 184. For a discussion of a theology of death in Judaism, see pp. 167–218.
11 Cited by Carse, ibid., p. 133.
12 For a discussion of the concept of death in Buddhism, see Carse, ibid., pp. 136–64.
13 See Carse's discussion of the concept of death in Plato, ibid., pp. 11–31.
14 *In Search of Humanity* (New York: Crossroad Publishing, 1983), pp. 241–2.
15 *Being and Time*, pp. 310–11.
16 *Is There an Answer to Death?* (Englewood Cliffs, NJ: Prentice-Hall, 1976), pp. 7, 10–11, 33.
17 *Death and Eternal Life*, (San Francisco: Harper and Row, 1962) p. 413.
18 *Death and Existence*, p. 10.
19 *Freedom and Death* (London: Chaucer Publishing, 1973), pp. 164–5; 168. Readers interested in further exposition of Heidegger's thought with regard to death can find it in Jacques

Choron, *Death and Western Thought* (New York: Collier Books, 1963), pp. 234–40. Choron also has a helpful exposition of the existentialist views on death by Sartre, pp. 246–54, including a discussion of the differences between Heidegger and Sartre. Carse's *Death and Existence* has a careful and perceptive exposition of Heidegger's views on death, pp. 410–31. For a trenchant criticism of Heidegger as well as of existentialist views on death from a historicist perspective, see Gordon Kaufman's 'Existentialism and Death', in *The Meaning of Death*, edited by Herman Feifel. Additional critical reflections upon existentialist interpretations of death can be found in the essay by Joseph Haroutunian, 'Life and Death Among Fellowmen', in *The Modern Vision of Death*, Nathan A. Scott, Jr (Richmond, VA: John Knox Press, 1967), pp. 85ff; *Death: an Interdisciplinary Analysis*, by Warren Shibles (Whitewater, WI: Language Press, University of Wisconsin, 1974), pp. 81–145.

20 Cited by J. Choron, *Death and Western Thought*, pp. 60, 102.
21 *Death: The Riddle and the Mystery*, pp. 14, 15.
22 *Act and Being* (London: Collins, 1962). p. 80.
23 *Creation and Fall* (London: SCM Press, 1959), p. 51.
24 *Letters and Papers From Prison* (New York: Macmillan, 1972), p. 312.
25 *Living With Death*, p. 189.
26 *Death: The Riddle and the Mystery*, p. 42.
27 Cited by Thielicke, *Living With Death*, p. 18.
28 *The Facts of Death* (Englewood Cliffs, NJ: Prentice-Hall, 1979), p. 5.

CHAPTER 2

Death and the Contemporary Mind

We no longer think about the dead, we think about dying. The dead are removed from us surreptitiously. One moment there is the dying, under the care of licensed professionals who grant us occasional intrusions into the process. The next moment, there is an empty bed, an empty room, and no further need to make the anxious visit to hospital. The one who is now dead has disappeared, under the care of licensed professionals, and only emerges for a fleeting moment, if at all, as an artefact in the liturgical drama supervised by a team of professional caretakers.

In America the dead are now surrendered to the assured peace of 'perpetual care' in a professionally maintained and landscaped park, where no children play and no 'communion with the saints' occurs on a casual Sunday afternoon. In a grotesque caricature of Jesus' aphorism, we 'leave the dead to think about the dead' and go on our way thinking about dying.[1]

How did this happen? How did our concern for the dead become a concern for death, and then for dying?

As we probe deeper into this phenomenon, discussion will focus on two areas: first, several aspects of the contemporary mind with respect to death will be examined, including some changing perspectives on our understanding of death; and secondly, several issues which are critical for a contemporary understanding of death will be highlighted.

There is an avoidance of death in our contemporary western culture. How do we account for this?

Some have explained this phenomenon as a kind of 'Victorian' repression of death in the same way that sex was repressed in an earlier age. This was the analysis in Geoffrey

Gorer's 1965 essay on 'The Pornography of Death'.[2] Death has become the great 'taboo', replacing sex. So thinks Malcolm Muggeridge: 'For most contemporary minds the notion of death is hidden away, unmentioned if not unmentionable, as the Victorians hid away the notion of sex.'[3]

Bernard Kalish echoes the same theme:

> Death is blasphemous and pornographic. We react to it and its symbols in the same way as we react to any pornography. We avoid it. We deny it exists. We avert our eyes from its presence. We protect little children from observing it and dodge their questions about it. We speak of it only in whispers. We consider it horrible, ugly and grotesque.[4]

Helmut Thielicke thinks that the modern mind's inability to think of death is because it has come to represent the 'final taboo'. While he also relates the contemporary avoidance of death to the same kind of taboo which once existed with regard to sex, he probes deeper into this phenomenon than simply calling it a form of pornography.

There is in death, says Thielicke, a deep mystery and even a quasi-occultic power which must be masked off from our direct observation and encounter. Thus, while there is a taboo about death which conceals its terror, there is also a profound interest and curiosity which attracts us to it. What we really fear in meeting death directly, says Thielicke, may be the encounter with ourselves as unknown people, and this may cause us greater fear than the thought of an unknown hereafter or of the nothingness of the night of death.[5]

I believe that Thielicke points us to the truth in this case. Human beings have always clothed their deepest mysteries in taboos. The function of a taboo is not the same as that of pornography. Pornography is a taboo which has become secularized and which has lost its mystery.

The avoidance of death in our contemporary society does not mean that death has become irrelevant. Out of sight does not, in this case, mean out of mind.

There is still something 'uncanny' about death, particularly about the dead person. For we are not sure just what we mean by a 'dead person,' after all. Thomas Aquinas was known to have expressed the opinion that even though a physical organism remains, this is not enough to say that a person remains. To say 'flesh and bones' may be meaningful, but in the strict sense it is no longer possible to speak of a 'hand'. Only a living, animated hand is really a hand at all.[6]

There is a heavy silence, even a conspiracy, which surrounds death. The physicians are not the villains in this conspiracy, even though, as Thielicke reminds us, 'The death of patients is thus felt to be a personal defeat. Doctors are like attorneys who lose cases and are thus forced to face up to the limit of their own powers. No wonder that they conceal their faces and turn aside!'[7]

There is a more profound reason for this 'conspiracy of silence' which surrounds death than the awkwardness of professional failure. There is what William May once called the 'sacral power' of death. Despite the prevailing secularism of the contemporary mind, says May, this silence and avoidance of death is evidence of the very sacred event with which death confronts us, unavoidably.[8]

There is an immensity about death which transcends the biological event of cessation of organic life. The rituals of evasion which surround the contemporary avoidance of death are not because death is considered trivial or incidental, but because we feel an inner sense of bankruptcy before this sacred, and impenetrable immensity. Thus, says May, 'The attempts at evasion and concealment are pathetic rather than casual.'[9]

The sacred is concealed in silence, but experienced in ritual. In the positive sense, the taboo preserves this sacred silence while also providing access to the mystery it conceals. The reality of God for the Jew was concealed in the name which was unutterable. Jahweh was the unspoken name of the God who was experienced through the history of their temporal lives – suspended between the biological events of birth and death. The very name Jahweh is taboo, especially because it signifies a relation which is familiar and intimate.

In somewhat the same way, we might understand the ambivalence with regard to death in our contemporary society. On the one hand there is a turning of our thoughts away from the dead and death by the removal of death from the rituals of our public and family life. We no longer have to think about death because we no longer actually see it.

On the other hand, there is a fascination and preoccupation with the philosophical and psychological implications and experiences of dying. Death is no longer taboo, it has been demythologized of its sacred power and has become the legitimate subject of academic study, as the proliferation of courses on Thanatology and Death and Dying in the universities now gives witness. In a society in which religion has been systematically turned into self help programmes for successful living, death and the dead have been surrendered to those who are licensed by the state. The death certificate has replaced the death watch.

There is then a fundamental ambivalence about death for the contemporary person. Death has been pushed out of sight and out of the context of daily life. No longer is death itself a meaningful ritual of family or social life. Yet, there is the emergence of a quite specific awareness of death as an existential concern quite apart from the event of death itself.

Strangely enough, awareness of death in the form of the psychological effects of death as a condition of life has grown in inverse proportion to the silence concerning death itself. Where death was once the unspoken word that accompanied communion with and commitment to the dead as a ritual of public and community life, there was virtually no literature on death and dying.

Today, death is not merely the unspoken word that surrounds the sacred power of death as an experienced event of life, but death has been translated into dying and the silence has been broken. One author has stated that he has reviewed over 800 books on death and dying, and has more than 2,000 articles in his files on the same subject![10]

For all of this robust interest in the subject of death and dying, it is also true that our western culture has lost its fundamental connection with death itself. The individual no longer presides over his or her death, as was common in the biblical practice and continued in many ways through the medieval period. The family no longer participates in the ritual of dying. These rituals have now become restricted to monitoring bodily functions, administering chemical substances and connecting with artificial life support systems, all under the supervision of medical professionals. Death has become institutionalized and professionalized. Religious professionals, on the other hand, develop their own techniques on ministering to the psychological needs of the dying, and providing grief counselling to the survivors.

Contrasted with this separation of society from the dead and the dying, is the fact that we are also a society that views more simulated deaths on television in a few days than most of our ancestors confronted real deaths in a life-time! In a report to the American Academy of Pediatrics in 1971, we were told that by the time a child in the United States reaches the age of 14 he or she can be expected to have seen, on average, 18,000 people killed on television![11] Yet, these same children will live, on average, for the next 40 years without experiencing the death or loss of an immediate family member. And even then, they will be shielded from the death so that the living will disappear instantly, almost like the sudden departure of a character in a television drama.

These are generalizations, to be sure, and many exceptions can be found. But in the main, I believe that no one would dispute this depiction of the contemporary situation. Death as an actual event has been separated from family and public life. We do not want to think about death, nor do we want to deal directly with it. While there has arisen an awareness of death as part of the psychology of life, and a body of literature concerning the psychology of dying, there is no place for death in the contemporary person's world view.

We must realize, however, that this is a phenomenon quite peculiar to our western culture, and that it is a quite recent trend. Several factors have been cited as contributing to this situation. Some have attributed the origin of the modern 'death-denying' culture to the Enlightenment emphasis on the glorifying of life and the creation of a new 'humanism' in which death was relegated to the lower, biological order of existence.[12]

John Hick suggests that the sources of the contemporary situation with regard to the dichotomy between death and life are rooted in the materialism which resulted from 'western science-oriented Humanism.' The world and man, says Hick, are now considered to be no more than a part of the phenomenon of nature, with human life a product of biological evolution, where individuals perish absolutely at death like all other organisms of the species. Hick himself, of course, does not agree with this view.[13]

Some attribute this phenomenon to the post-Enlightenment denial of individual immortality by atheistic and sceptical eighteenth century philosophers and scientists, with a turn towards naturalism, positivism and Marxism. Russell Aldwinckle goes so far as to say that Bertrand Russell, 'More than any other single man, particularly in the English-speaking countries, has been responsible for the modern distrust of human desires'.[14]

Aldwinckle cites Russell's book, *A Free Man's Worship*, as the most eloquent statement of his conviction that we must face honestly and openly the ultimate and total extinction of the human race and yet continue to live courageously on the basis of unyielding despair. As evidence that this philosophy of despair with regard to life after death has been taken into theological discourse, Aldwinckle points to the historicism in the theology of Gordon Kaufmann, as one who accepts the philosophy of natural humanism with death as the final event in the life of the individual.[15]

Is it helpful to look for the sources of our modern preoccupation with the avoidance of death and to assign blame to any one person or movement? Probably not. The main concern here has been to identify the role which death plays for the contemporary person. Death has been edged out of the rituals of common life and relegated to the realm of the invisible world from which we are protected by the discrete skills of the professionals.

How then is death viewed by the social scientists and the medical specialists who see it in abstraction from the rituals of human life itself? Rather pragmatically, it appears. It is an inevitable biological and natural fact of life. Human life is a moving sea of faces and forces, no longer subject to the whims of the gods. Technology and the human sciences have become the instruments by which we westerners navigate over this open sea. Is it possible that death may be as much a pragmatic solution to life as a tormenting problem?

'The spirit of Western culture', writes Kenneth Vaux, 'which is the spirit of scientific medicine, is today an erratic wind that cannot sustain full-blown the sails of our technological voyage'.[16] There is a fundamental ambivalence in what we think about death. Distinguished scientists at the World Food Conference in Rome suggested that perhaps famine should take its course among the peoples of India and Africa.

Garrett Hardin, the distinguished biologist, is one who speaks from the more radical end of this continuum. Only rarely is death a social tragedy, he argues, 'death need not be a personal tragedy; and it is abundantly clear that death will always fulfil an important, even essential, role in human society. In fact, it is hard to escape concluding that the social importance of death will become even greater in the foreseeable future.'[17]

Noting the way in which philosophers who write on the subject of death contradict one another, Hardin cites Pascal as saying: 'There is nothing more real than death, nor more terrible.' But then he also cites Spinoza in response: 'A free man thinks of nothing less than of death; and his wisdom is a meditation not of death, but of life.'[18] Hardin, of course, agrees with Spinoza and wonders that Pascal, so good a mathematician, could have spawned so much nonsense in philosophy as to say that death is real when death actually is a kind of zero, and zero, therefore, cannot be a real number! Rational people, concludes Hardin, should not fear death; and when it appears inevitable, they should hasten it.

The spirit of western culture is indeed an erratic wind, as Vaux has reminded us. As a scientist, Hardin can look death squarely in the eye and see it as a natural, and even necessary element of our social environment. He can 'think death', so to speak, but primarily as an abstraction. We do not know how he thinks his own death. There is ample evidence that there is another wind blowing in our western culture, and that it is the prevailing wind. In this direction, we do not really think death at all, even abstractly, and even the dead are removed from our vision as aesthetically as possible. Instead, we focus on our awareness of death as personal and existential loss, and attempt to find meaning in that experience.

So here we have come full circle. We began by asserting the thesis that death is something to be avoided, and even concealed for the contemporary person. If it is no more than a biological inevitability, it may also be a pragmatic necessity. Yet there remains a strand of the contemporary psyche which refuses to be comforted by such pragmatic realism. The problem of death refuses to be buried by concealment or neutralized by pragmatic abstractions.

The French philosopher Gabriel Marcel, who became a

Roman Catholic in 1929, and who, one could assume, had thereby found the answer to the problem of death, replied: 'there is a part of me which is not yet evangelized' to explain his continued preoccupation with the theme of death. Yet, when chided for attaching too much importance to his own death, Marcel replied, 'what counts is not my death, not yours, but the death of those we love'. The problem, for Marcel, continued to be the essential conflict between love and death as an existential theme. To love another, he asserted, is to say 'you shall not die'.[19]

Before we leave this discussion of the contemporary mind as it views death in its own ambivalent way, we need to remember that we have only been looking at death from the the rather parochial perspective of our western world. We are contemporaries of quite a different world view, represented by non-western cultures and philosophies.

Non-western cultures have, by and large, retained the original power of cosmologies, religious systems and philosophies in which death is not seen as the absolute end of existence. In these world views, consciousness, or life in some form, continues beyond the point of physical death. These systems, while ranging from concepts of the afterlife which contain highly abstract levels of (impersonal) consciousness to images of otherworld existence which resemble earthly forms, none the less, hold in common that death is transitional and a bridge to a further stage.

For the Hindu, unenlightened life appears to be a state of separation, imprisonment and delusion, whereas death is reunion, spiritual liberation and awakening. Death represents an opportunity for the individual self (jiva) to break away from worldly illusion (maya) and experience its divine nature (Atman–Brahman).

In cultures where reincarnation plays a significant role, such as Hinduism, Jainism and Tibetan Tantrism, dying may be viewed as more important than living. For the Buddhist, suffering is intrinsic to biological existence. The ultimate goal of the individual is thus a spiritual pilgrimage, which gradually extinguishes the fire of (physical) life and frees the individual from the wheel of death and rebirth. Dying is seen as a step in the spiritual or cosmological hierarchy, a promotion into the world of revered ancestors, powerful spirits or demigods. Many of these traditions include the belief that one can do no better to prepare for death than acquire intellectual knowledge of the process of dying.

The individual dying in such a culture, whether an ancient, pre-industrial one or a contemporary one, is thus equipped with a religious or philosophical system that transcends death and which can offer experiential training in altered states of consciousness, including symbolic confrontations with death. The approach to death may even be accompanied by the nourishing context of extended family, clan or tribe, and even include specific guidance through the successive stages of dying.[20]

In contrast to this, as we have seen, the typical western view of death has become more pragmatic and dissociated from religious or philosophical worldviews. Ageing and dying are not seen as integral parts of the life process, but as reminders of our limited ability to control nature, despite technological and scientific achievements in this regard. The educated westerner tends to regard belief in consciousness after death as a manifestation of primitive fears and relics of religion. Nietzsche even went so far as to say that fear of death is a 'European disease', and attributed it largely to the influence of Christianity.[21]

The empirical sciences explain death in terms of mechanistic and organic processes. In the Cartesian–Newtonian world-view, which prevails in western society, consciousness is the product of the brain and thus ceases at the time of physical death. This view has only recently been challenged by scientists such as Sir John Eccles who argues that self consciousness, while a component of the empirical phenomena, cannot be reduced to an effect produced by the physical elements of the brain.[22]

In order to provide the dying with the maximum benefits of scientific medical research and technology, the dying person is usually institutionalized under the assumption that the vital processes of life are essentially organic and physical. The discontinuity experienced with the breaking off of relations between the dying person and the family and community is not considered to be a threat to the vital life process.

Only recently have there occurred changes in our approach to death through the recognition that dying, like giving birth,

is a vital life function that includes the network of relationships that contribute to the value and quality of life. The
development of the hospice movement, for example, is but one
such indication of a reversal of the trend towards the
depersonalizing and dehumanizing of death. Recent research
into the phenomenon of clinical death and near-death experiences has opened up new interest in the area of consciousness
during and after death. Hitherto, the possibility of consciousness after death had tended to be rejected not because it
contradicted clinical observations, but *a priori* because the
concept was incompatible with existing scientific theories.[23]

I have tried up to this point to draw a profile of the
contemporary mind with regard to death. I have sketched this
profile in broad strokes, making generalizations, while at the
same time pointing to some evidence of a changing perspective
on death. Yet, these changes themselves are evidence for a
prevailing attitude by their very exceptional nature.

In summary, we can say this about death in our contemporary western society. Our attention is not fixed upon the dead
nor upon death. We no longer are capable of sustaining the
taboo of death within our rituals of life in a positive sense of
being in touch with the 'sacral power of death'. We are living
longer, dying older and more slowly, and yet the only death
that most of us will really experience directly is our own.
Having compartmentalized death so that we no longer live in
continuity with the dead, we are none the less preoccupied
with an awareness of death such as never before. While we
have surrendered the clinical side of death to the medical
scientists and the human side of death to the social theorists,
there remain issues with regard to death which are of a
philosophical, psychological and religious nature.

It is to these issues that this chapter now turns. To state the
issues directly:

1 What definition do we give to death, and how does our
   definition of death determine our ethical responsibility to
   the dying? This is a philosophical issue.
2 Given our increasing awareness of death, what does this
   mean in terms of mental health and the quality of life?
   This is a psychological issue.
3 If God no longer guards the threshold of eternal life at the
   gateway of death, can we continue to speak of personal

immortality as a sustaining reality of life? This is a religious issue.

While these implications will concern us throughout the rest of this book, each of them must be touched on briefly in this context.

We cannot think of death at all without being aware of the philosophical problems which immediately arise. When we use a word like 'death', we have to decide what we mean by it. One of the functions of philosophy is to clarify concepts so that the words we use do not confuse the issue itself.[24]

Peter Koestenbaum argues that the very fact that the state, or government, takes over the responsibility for certifying death and licensing healers (biologists) means that the 'State has entered the field of philosophy and ruled on truth'.[25] This is not to suggest that a society should be prevented from regulating the practice of healing, as it does the practice of disposing of the dead; but the philosophical issue involved is the definition of the meaning of the event which is thereby subject to regulation.

If the prevailing definition of life in our scientific western culture is materialistic then the working definition of death will be one derived from clinical observation of the process by which that life degenerates and ceases to exist as a biological phenomenon. The naiveté which once permitted the mystery of death to be embraced as a 'taboo' and incorporated into the rituals of the living community permitted very 'rough and ready' definitions of the point of death. A new order of priests has arisen who serve the god of natural law. No longer is the old naiveté permitted in the examination room. The organic life functions of human persons are now known to be complex and interrelated. Vital life processes yield their secrets to those who understand the principles of causality inherent in the organic system.

But with the loss of naiveté there has also been the loss of mystery. The only secrets are those which exist within the new order of priests who stand in a mysterious relationship to the uninitiated and untrained lay person. What surgery fails to remedy, an autopsy discloses to the surgeon. Every death has to have a biological cause; it is no longer permitted to be a secret.

With the advances in scientific technology during the past

several decades, one would think that precision and a high degree of certainty would now be possible in defining the exact point of death.

The exact opposite now seems to be the case. Responsibility for determining the exact point of clinical death remains a human decision based on criteria which include, but are not limited to, the biological, neuro-electrical and molecular components of the human body. Technically, the human body 'dies several deaths' in the process of degeneration. Which of these 'deaths' should be considered the death of the person? The bodily organs, at least as molecular forms of living cells, survive the death of the human person. This is recognized in all modern definitions of clinical death.

But what then is a human person? What does death remove from the human organism which constitutes loss of person-hood? And how is this understood as a loss of life, when there are certain biological functions which continue for a time after the point of clinical death is determined? And if a decision is to be made in any case, what perspective on life and death informs this decision? No longer is it as simple as saying that a person is dead when the vital signs of life disappear.

These questions have led some to suggest that the concept of death is not only multidisciplinary but also heavily philosophical in content.[26] We should thus distinguish between a *concept* of death and *criteria* for defining death in a clinical setting. In thinking of a concept of death, the underlying issue is the nature of person. Attempts to determine the point of death through clinical criteria alone have become increasingly complicated and unsatisfying. A concept of person underlies the use of criteria for determining life and death decisions. Obviously this is a philosophical issue and not merely a matter of accurate clinical observation.

A traditional American legal definition of death, written in 1890, is 'the cessation of life; the ceasing to exist defined by physicians as a total stoppage of the circulation of the blood, and a cessation of the animal and vital functions consequent thereon, such as respiration, pulsation' and so on.[27] One hardly need comment on the inadequacy of this in light of more recent advances in the ability to sustain persons on life support systems and even to resuscitate those who have appeared clinically dead for some minutes.

More recently, the State of Kansas, in 1971, adopted a statute which attempts to define clinical death in accordance with more elaborate criteria and ends with the noteworthy sentence: 'Death is to be pronounced before artificial means of supporting respiratory and circulatory function are terminated and before any vital organ is removed for the purpose of transplantation.'[28] With the proliferation of organ transplants, including the implantation of the heart of a baboon in the body of newly born infant in California, the definition of death as well as the definition of life, clearly assumes ethical and philosophical proportions.

These cases are cited only to make the following point. The concept of death becomes increasingly complex and difficult when we are limited to criteria which are derived out of an unrelenting materialist view of life coupled with the pragmatism of a scientific/technological medical community of professional technicians. This 'cadaverization' of life, as Jacques Choron has put it, is a surrender of the consecration of life to the impersonal criteria of death as an event within the materialist world.[29]

If indeed the concept of person is crucial to the application of criteria for defining death, then the definition of death is itself of theological and philosophical concern. For what is at stake is our concept of the human person. We shall have more to say about this in the following chapter.

A second issue concerning our understanding of death can be seen as more psychological then philosophical. Though the boundaries are not always clear in this regard, we are reminded by Peter Koestenbaum that current interest in death originated with the existential philosophers and has been taken over by psychologists. Death is a philosophical issue, he remarks, 'and psychologists did not start talking about its therapeutic importance until the existential philosophers pointed out to them that it was important to do so'.[30]

None the less, we feel that there are aspects relating to death for the contemporary person which are genuinely psychological. These aspects have to do with the mental health of those who live with conscious, or even repressed fear of death. There are also aspects to the problem of death which relate to the psychological health and strength of those who are dying.

Certainly one aspect of the preoccupation with death which

is symptomatic of our western culture is the awareness of death which occurs in the form of anxiety or fear of death, or in the neurotic forms of repression and denial of death. The existential philosophers tend to view this awareness of death as a clue to the meaning of life. The concern for psychology, on the other hand, is more for the therapeutic clues which awareness of death and fear of death can provide as a movement towards health.

Ernest Becker blends these two concerns when he discusses denial of death as the core of most neuroses (contrary to Freud) and at the same time suggests that faith in God is the most viable way to live with this fear of death and so achieve mental health. His Pulitzer Prize winning book *The Denial of Death* was published shortly before his own death from cancer.[31]

Becker describes the 'healthy-minded' person as one who insists that fear of death is an acquired instinct. This person maintains that we are born with a natural confidence in life. Our anxiety and dread result from nurture and not from nature. Becker himself does not subscribe to this view. He argues that the fear of death is intrinsic to our nature as persons and that all sickness of the soul is rooted in the denial and repression of this reality.

This denial takes the form of a heroic transference, by which one seeks to 'immortalize' the self by divinizing some object near at hand – or even the hand that manipulates the object. The larger canvas of life is really a portrait of our mortality, and we will expire before tracing out all of the possibilities that confront us. The 'normal' person survives by partializing life and narrowing that 'terrifying vision of life' by concentrating on an accessible object or manageable task. It is this task which then becomes the heroic endeavour.

Drawing upon the philosophical anthropology of Kierkegaard, Becker posits anxiety as the critical core of the self which, in becoming aware of itself as a self, is caught in an existential predicament. The immensity of life's possibilities as freedom of spirit offers a self transcendence which overcomes the boundary of the flesh and finitude. At the same time, awareness includes the inevitability of one's own finitude and mortality. The 'terror of being alive' is matched by the horror of inevitable death.

With penetrating insight (despite some tendency to fasten on the pathological aspect of this freedom), Becker shows that the reality of death reaches into every nook and cranny of life, casting a shadow over the cheerful play of the child as well as the optimistic and idealistic dreams of youth.

Becker would agree with Jung's statement that the diagnosis for 'good health' is 'mortal illness.'[32] The prognosis for good health is death. The human person is mortally stricken with life.

The pathological side of this 'denial of death', argues Becker, is neurosis. The neurotic partializes life in order to reduce the anxiety produced by the apparent limitless possibilities of life. At the same time, the neurotic seeks to overcome the awareness of mortality by some kind of project of self preservation, or, what he calls the tendency to immortalize the self. Applying this analysis to the history of psychoanalysis, Becker argues that mental illness and problems of neurotic behaviour can, for the most part, be traced to this core anxiety over death and the need to deny it.

The way out of this impasse, he suggests, is the movement of positive transference, or 'life enhancing illusion' by which one is cast on the transcending reality of a being which is able to sustain the human person in a continual state of reality. This movement he calls faith, following the direction of Kierkegaard.

Citing the psychoanalyst Otto Rank, who claimed that man was a 'theological being – not a biological one', Becker argues that religion and psychology come together in this analysis of the self.[33] There is a false, neurotic, heroism which cripples life and leads deeper into a denial of death and consequently a loss of the vital power of life. But there is also an authentic heroism, argues Becker, which can lead to the triumph of life over death and to a 'triumphant death'.

In his final paragraph, at the end of this enormously creative and perceptive book, Becker appears uncertain as to just what form this triumph will take.

> Who knows what form the forward momentum of life will take in the time ahead, or what use it will make of our anguished searching. The most that any one of us can seem to do is to fashion something – an object or ourselves – and drop it into the confusion, make an offering of it, so to speak, to the life force.

Yet, on his own death bed a few months later, in an interview with Sam Keen, Becker affirmed that he was not a Stoic, 'but I believe in God'. And this belief, he asserted, enabled him to

> feel a great sense of relief and trust that eggs are not hatched in vain. Beyond accident and contingency and terror and death there is a meaning that redeems, redeems not necessarily in personal immortality or anything like that but a redemption that makes it good somehow. And that is enough. . . I think it is very hard for secular men to die.[34]

In the end, Becker's nostalgic longing for something more lacks a convincing ring, despite his penetrating insights which expose the denial of death which lurks behind every facade that we create in order to seek immortality in the present. From the perspective of a Christian theology it is not enough to be asked to cling to a 'somehow' and 'someway' in which the anxiety of death can be transformed into comfort and hope.

In his psychologizing of death for the sake of creating a valid philosophy of life, Becker has thought about death more honestly and patiently than most of our contemporaries. His critique stands as a warning to the bastions of materialism and scientism that the human spirit will not yield to a definition of death which makes it only a matter of clinical concern at the end of life. At the same time, he has exposed the superficiality and downright unhealthiness of religious attempts to conceal the reality of death by promising immortality 'in the sweet bye and bye'.

Yet, in the end, his attempt to overcome the problem of death appears to falter. This may be shown in two ways. First, his concept of faith is based on too narrow a concept of the person. The razor-edge of existential anxiety does not take into account the essential social nature of the human person, nor does it have a view of health which is essentially pre-dates pathology of guilt and fear of death. There appears to be a fundamental ambivalence in Becker's anthropology. In an earlier work he clearly outlined the social structure of human existence as essential to a definition of the normal self, and as a means of affirming fundamental values to human life. Yet, even here he turns away from the concrete social structure of human selfhood to reach out for the abstract as a way of freeing oneself from this dependence upon the other.

The person has to learn to derive his self-esteem more from within himself and less from the opinion of others; . . . The value of deriving one's power and meaning from the highest level of generality is that it makes this task for the self-esteem easier; one can feel that he has ultimate value deep down inside just by serving in the cosmic hero-system: he has a sense of duty to the very powers of creation and not principally or only to the social world.[35]

Secondly, his attempt may be said to lack convincing power because he has not satisfied the essentially religious question which surrounds the question of death: does belief in God sustain the personal reality of life beyond death? Or, is God merely an abstraction which serves as an answer to the existential quest for transcendence? If it is the latter, then the reality of personal immortality has been thrown into the existential limbo of faith for the sake of a therapeutic placebo. Christian theology places its hope for immortality on the concrete and historical event of Jesus' resurrection from the dead. Personal immortality consists not in attaching oneself to a supra-cosmic power, but in the hope of one's own resurrection from the dead through the power of God in Jesus Christ.

This leads us to the third issue in this analysis of death in our contemporary culture. When we think about death, what do we think about our own personal immortality? We cannot think about death without asking this profoundly religious question.

Apart from relation to God, says Helmut Thielicke, our death could not be a personal death and it could not be a human death. Thus far, Becker has been on the right track. But Thielicke also goes on to suggest that this human life (*zoe* as opposed to mere *bios*) remains exclusively under God's control, even when I 'sink into death'. Physical death is the 'biological mask' which, for all of its literalness, does not 'literally' destroy my life in partnership with God. I sink into death, says Thielicke, but not in such a way that I will stay in it, 'for God has called me by name and will call me again on his day. I am under the protection of the risen Lord no matter what anxiety the long night of death might cause. I am not immortal, but I am one who awaits the resurrection.'[36]

The question that emerges in the form of the religious

question when we think about death is that of immortality –
survival beyond death in some form that means continuity
with the present self. Discussion of immortality as a condition
of our present natural and temporal existence will have to wait
for the next chapter. It must be said at this point, however,
that when we think about death we unavoidably think about
our own desire for immortality; and this is true even if our
conclusion is to deny it. For a theory about death which denies
the immortality of the self beyond death has addressed the
religious issue with regard to death, not merely a philosophical
or psychological one.

The need for immortality can take many forms in our
culture. There is a certain attraction towards the eastern
concept of reincarnation, which at least offers a concept of
continuity, though not at the level of personal identity.
Perhaps the most pervasive and typical is the quasi-religious
hope that some project we have invested with our own life
energy will survive, and that, as Becker put it, 'eggs are not
hatched in vain'.

We must also take note of the fact that within this stream of
western culture, despite the day-to-day hard-headed realism of
our pragmatic, scientific and technological efforts, there still
exists the intellectual and traditional formulation of the
Christian message.

Easter has not yet surrendered its psychic hold on the
consciousness of the contemporary mind. Multitudes still
expect to hear a Christian answer to Job's ancient question: 'If
a man die shall he live again?' (Job 14:14). But not all will
remember that this question put by Job was preceded by his
melancholy lament:

> Man that is born of woman is of few days,
>   and full of trouble.
> He comes forth like a flower, and withers;
> He flees like a shadow, and continues not. (14:1–2)

Or, as the Psalmist has said: 'What is man that thou art
mindful of him' (Psalm 8:4).

The question about death is not merely about death itself,
but about human death. What is it about human death that
leads Christian theology to conclude that it is a consequence of
sin? This is the question to be addressed in the following
chapter.

NOTES

1   Charles Jackson comments with insight on the disappearance in America of the rural cemetery in favour of modern park-like settings where 'perpetual care' is offered without need for personal commitment to the dead on the part of survivors. 'Death Shall Have no Dominion: The Passing of the World of the Dead in America', in *Death and Dying – Views from Many Cultures*, edited by Richard A. Kalish (Farmdale, NY: Baywood Publishing, 1979), p. 51.

2   *Death, Grief and Mourning* (Garden City, NY: Doubleday, 1965).

3   *Observer* (20 February 1970). Cited in *Will to Live/Will to Die*, by Kenneth Vaux (Minneapolis: Augsburg Publishing, 1978), p. 13.

4   'Some Variables in Death Attitudes', in *Death and Identity*, edited by Robert Fulton (New York: John Wiley, 1965). A similar view is expressed by Ronald C. Starenko, *God, Grass, and Grace: A Theology of Death* (St Louis, MO: Concordia Publishing, 1975), pp. 12ff. Kenneth L. Vaux also accounts for the repression of death in the minds of many as a 'new pornography' *Will to Live/Will to Die*, pp. 12ff. So also does William May in his essay, 'The Sacral Power of Death in Contemporary Experience', in *Perspectives on Death*, edited by Liston O. Mills, Nashville: Abingdon Press, 1969), pp. 172ff.

5   *Living With Death*, (Grand Rapids, Eerdmans, 1983), pp. 29ff.

6   Cited by Josef Pieper, *Death and Immortality* (New York: Herder and Herder, 1969), p. 45.

7   *Living With Death*, p. 44.

8   'The Sacral Power of Death in Contemporary Experience', pp. 168ff.

9   Ibid., p. 170.

10 Michael Simpson, *The Facts of Death* (Englewood Cliffs, NJ: Prentice-Hall, 1979), pp. 5, 264. At the end of this book, Simpson produces a select bibliography arranged by topic. For a bibliography citing over 400 titles, see John Hick, *Death and Eternal Life* (San Francisco: Harper and Row, 1976), pp. 467–81. Perhaps the most extensive general bibliography of the literature on death and dying can be found in *Death: An Interdisciplinary Analysis*, by Warren Shibles (Whitewater, WI: Language Press, 1974), pp. 525–58, with over 1,500 titles listed. A bibliography of works related more to the technical and scientific factors in death and dying can be found in *On Defining Death: An Analytic Study of the Concept of Death in Philosophy and Medical Ethics*, by Douglas N. Walton (Montreal: McGill-Queen's University Press, 1979), pp. 167–86. One of the better selected bibliographies on

death, dying and bereavement has been published by Leonard Pearson in *Death and Dying – Current Issues in the Treatment of the Dying Person* (Cleveland and London: Case Western Reserve University Press, 1969), pp. 133–235. This is an annotated bibliography, arranged in ten categories, and covering more than 650 listings.

11 Cited by Hick, *Death and Eternal Life*, p. 86.

12 This is the view held by Liston Mills, for example, in *Perspectives on Death*, p. 8.

13 *Death and Eternal Life*, p. 437.

14 *Death in the Secular City*, (Grand Rapids: Eerdmans, 1972), p. 24.

15 Ibid., pp. 29, 37ff.

16 *Will to Live/Will to Die*, p. 53.

17 *Promethean Ethics* (Seattle and London: University of Washington Press, 1980), p. 19.

18 Ibid., pp. 23–4.

19 Cited by Choron, *Death and Western Thought* (New York: Collier, 1963), pp. 254–6.

20 Much of the above has been drawn from the helpful analysis provided by Stanislav and Christina Grof, *Beyond Death: The Gates of Consciousness* (New York: Thames and Hudson, 1980), pp. 5–7. Cf. also John Hick's extensive discussion of eastern views of death and dying, *Death and Eternal Life*, pp. 297–398; also, *Death and Dying: Views from Many Cultures*, edited by Richard A. Kalish (Farmdale, NY: Baywood Publishing, 1979); also, *The Last Enemy*, by Richard Wolff (Washington, DC: Canon Press, 1974), pp. 34–41.

21 Cited by Richard Wolff, *The Last Enemy*, p. 15. Wolff also cites David Cole Gordon as holding the view that the dark feelings of fear in the face of death, far from being diminished by religion, are enhanced by them, particularly by Christianity because of its alleged premise that only life hereafter really counts: *Overcoming the Fear of Death* (Baltimore: Penguin Books, 1972), p. 20.

22 *Facing Reality* (London: Heidelberg Science Library, 1970); cf. also, *The Human Mystery* (Berlin/Heidelberg: Springer-Verlag, 1979).

23 This is the conclusion drawn by Stanislav and Christina Grof, *Beyond Death*, pp. 8ff. We shall look more closely at some of these phenomena later.

24 The warning of Ludwig Wittgenstein is appropriate here: 'Philosophy is a battle against the bewitchment of our intelligence by means of language.' *Philosophical Investigations* (Oxford: Basil Blackwell, 1953), p. 47 (109).

25 *Is There an Answer to Death?* (Englewood Cliffs, NJ: Prentice-Hall, 1976), pp., 9–10.

26   Douglas Walton, *On Defining Death*, p. 18.
27   Cited by Michael Simpson, *The Facts of Death*, p. 18.
28   Ibid., p. 19. For further information on specific guidelines prepared for determining clinical death see, Kenneth Vaux, 'Death in Modern Medicine', in *Will to Live/Will to Die*, pp. 21–49. Also, 'Legal and Medical Definitions', in *On Defining Death*, by Douglas Walton, pp. 25–40.
29   *Death and Western Thought*, p. 258.
30   *Is There an Answer to Death?*, pp. 7, 32.
31   *The Denial of Death* (New York: Free Press, 1973).
32   Cited in Koestenbaum, *Is There an Answer to Death*, p.71.
33   *The Denial of Death*, p. 175.
34   *Psychology Today* (April, 1974), p. 78. For a critique of Becker's book, with a discussion of his place alongside Jaspers, Marcel, Tolstoi and Kierkegaard, see *God, Guilt, and Death: An Existential Phenomenology of Religion*, Merold Westphal (Bloomington: Indiana University Press, 1984), esp. 'The Existential Meaning of Death', pp. 90-106.
35   *The Birth and Death of Meaning: An Interdisciplinary Perspective on the Problem of Man*, (New York: Free Press, 1971), p. 192.
36   *Living With Death*, pp. 138, 163.

CHAPTER 3

Towards a Theology of Human Death

Socrates could have escaped death, and Jesus could have eased Pilate out of his predicament. Yet Socrates would not accept Crito's advice to leave town, and Jesus looked Pilate squarely in the eye and said, 'You could have no power over me unless it had been given you from above' (John 19:11).

Both Jesus and Socrates had a theology of death which was the logical outcome of their theology of life.

Socrates, as Plato tells the story, scoffed at the suggestion of his friends that he pay a small bribe and thereby escape death. 'You are mistaken', he told them, 'if you think that a man who is worth anything ought to spend his time weighing up the prospects of life and death. He has only one thing to consider in performing any action; that is, whether he is acting rightly or wrongly.'

'True philosophers', Socrates continued, 'make dying their profession.'[1]

The 'rehearsal of death' which characterizes the philosophy of Socrates is the process of perfecting the soul in its true knowledge of the eternal. Life and death were viewed as opposites, and because death had no power to extinguish the soul, but rather liberated it so that it might return whence it came, the life of the soul is eternal and rooted in the life of the divine. Hence, Socrates' theology of death is the logical outcome of his theology of the immortal soul.

Jesus, on the other hand, did not face his death with the equanimity of soul that characterizes the death of Socrates. 'Now is my soul troubled,' cried out Jesus, 'And what shall I say? 'Father save me from this hour?' No, for this purpose I have come to this hour. Father glorify thy name' (John 12:27, 28).

For Jesus, life and death are not logical opposites as they are for Socrates. Life and death both belong to that existence which issues from God. Therefore both life and death are subject to divine authority. 'Do not fear those who kill the body but cannot kill the soul,' Jesus had already taught, 'rather fear him who can destroy both soul and body in Gehenna (hell)' (Matthew 10:28).

These represent two approaches to death, because they represent two contrasting theologies of life. In the Greek tradition, which has found its way into some forms of Christian theology, death is a friend, for it marks the transition for our 'going to God'. In the Hebrew tradition, which informs Jesus' theology of life, death is a natural limitation to our earthly existence. This is God's determination of the form of life. Apart from relation to God as the one who sustains life for human persons, death becomes an enemy, as is clearly pointed out in the New Testament (Romans 5:12).[2]

It is the purpose of this chapter to develop a Christian theology of death. To do that, we will look first of all at the biblical teaching concerning life and death. Then we will examine some theological concerns which emerge out of this brief study. These concerns have to do with (1) the nature of human personhood and death, (2) death as an original aspect of human nature and (3) what we believe concerning the immortality of the human self.

There is no clearly defined theology of death in the Bible. This is surprising to us until we look more closely at the way in which the Bible deals with death.

While the Bible takes death seriously, it does not develop a theology of death. The theme of death is expressed descriptively (as history), poetically (as lamentation and complaint), theologically (as the outcome of sin) and eschatologically (as overcome through the resurrection of Jesus Christ). Yet, there is no single 'theology of death' to be found as a thematic development.

In the Old Testament we find references to death which are not directly related to questions of life. The Israelites experienced death as a reality at every step. What is remarkable, is that this did not cause them to seek an explanation for death in either psychological or religious terms. Even the attribution of death to the first fatal sin by Adam is no explanation of death.

This only states the theological relation between sin and death.

Rather, we find the concern of the Hebrews for life, particularly life as an expression of relation to Jahweh. Life is good; it is the highest of goods. A long life is a fulfilled life (Genesis 15:15; Judges 8:32; Job 42:17). Life rewarded by an assured posterity (Psalms 127; 128) is the highest gift that God can offer. Life is a blessing, not a curse (Deuteronomy 30:19).

Behind this is the understanding that God himself is the Living One (Deuteronomy 5:26; 2 Kings 19:4; Psalms 42:3), and that he is the fountain of life (Psalms 36:9). The Israelite vows, 'As the Lord lives' (Judges 8:19), and Jahweh swears by his own life (Numbers 14:21). In the Bible God is not the God of the dead, but of the living (Cf. Exodus 3:6; 16; Mark 12:27).

God's breath gives life to all that lives, and when He withdraws it, the creature is reduced to nothingness (Psalms 104:29f). Whatever the situation of the dead may be, and that is quite ambiguous, the terrible thing which has happened to them is that they are now excluded from the community of those who praise Jahweh (Psalms 6:5; 30:9; 88:10–12; 115:17; Isaiah 38:18ff).

Thus, the one who is physically alive, but who suffers without God's response, and who is subject to the taunts of the enemy 'Where is your God?' cries out: 'As with a deadly wound in my body, my adversaries taunt me' (Psalms 42:10). To be isolated from God is already to be in the place of death. Thus, the realm of the dead (Sheol) penetrates the sphere of those physically still alive (cf. Psalms 107). It is in this sense that death not only is a place, but is also a power that extends over life.

Death is therefore a part of life viewed as existence before God. But it is the weakest form of that life. It represents the attenuation of that vital life force which integrates soul and body. This life force is not a power that one has as a natural endowment, but one that is itself derived out of a relation to Jahweh.[4]

Death is the scattering of one's vital powers, a pouring out of the soul (Isaiah 53:12; Job 30:16). One who dies is like water spilled on the ground, not to be gathered up again (2 Samuel 14:14). In the underworld, in Sheol, there is no real life, even though persons continue to 'exist' as shadows of the real self.

There is no praise of God in Sheol, and the dead have no memory of the living (cf. Psalms 6:5).[5]

This Hebrew understanding of death as a shadow side of the community of the living can be explained, says Professor Wheeler Robinson, in the idea of the corporate personality of Israel as the essential unit of life, rather than individual personality. So long as family, clan and Israel lived, the shadow of life was cast even in the form of the dead, though it was not viewed as existence because there was no 'praise of Jahweh' possible.[6] This needs to be balanced with the concept of the individual as a vital unity of body and soul, with the blood seen as the principle of vitality, along with the 'breath of life'. While the individual might perish as one's life is 'spilt out on the ground', one's existence is continued in the corporate identity of the tribe and clan.

This leads to an apparent ambivalence with regard to death and the individual in the Old Testament. The power of death has its limits, for it is God who kills and brings to life (1 Samuel 2:6). It is He who returns man to the dust (Psalms 90:3). On the other hand, there is a reticence towards death which is rooted in Israel's religion. Israel's God is the God of the living, not the dead. The dead are cut off from His hand (Psalms 88:6). Bodies are unclean and must be removed from the sphere of that which is consecrated to God (Leviticus 21:1; Numbers 19:16; Deuteronomy 21:23). Thus, the realm of the dead is set at a distance from God and Israel must pay heed to this distance.

On the one hand, death is human and natural, for it is part of God's determination for human nature and not merely a fate which has a power of its own over the human. To die at a ripe old age was not seen as something unnatural, but was something that one could take for granted (Job 5:26; Genesis 27:2; 46:30; 48:21; 50:24). This leads to the concept of a 'good death' which occurs in the natural course of human life. Every person could have this expectation, even though, in reality, it was often quite different.

Yet, on the other hand, death could appear as a threat to life and even unnatural or as a sign of judgement, and even a curse, even though this curse is that which man has originally caused to come upon himself (Genesis 2:17; 3:19). Death, as a result of sin, came to be viewed as an end to the spiritual life of fellowship with God, and not merely as a natural physical event. This is why Sheol is viewed as extending its power beyond its boundaries and reaching into the midst of man's happy life (Psalms 49:14–15; 89:48).

When death is premature, violent or through disease, it no longer has the character of a 'good death'. This is why death catches man like a fish in a net (Ecclesiastes 9:12), and entangles him (2 Samuel 22:6; Psalms 18:6). Death is insatiable, it gathers and unites all men and nations and has no regard for position or rank (Habakkuk 2:5; Proverbs 27:20). This is why death poses a constant and continual threat to life. Yet, death can also be considered a curse in light of the 'rainbow' of God's covenant promise. It is sometimes viewed as the dark side of the blessing. Apart from this relation of death as a curse to the blessing and promise of God, there is no view of death in the Old Testament as inherently evil.

So death *can* be a peaceful end to life, and thus part of the good of the human life. This is because the time of one's death is also determined by God. Death is not intrinsically a curse and an arbitrary power that stands over and against one's human life. Yet, it is also a threat to the very humanity of life because it separates the individual in three ways: from himself in the dissolution of the body and soul and loss of vital power; from the community by which the individual gains his identity; and from God, who is the very source of life itself.[7]

'He is the Lord of death,' writes Karl Barth, 'but this does not mean that He affirms it. As the Creator He affirms life and only life. . . His control over death is exercised for the sake of life and not for the sake of death. 'Have I any pleasure at all that the wicked should die? saith the Lord God: and not that he should return from his ways, and live?' (Ezekiel 18:23, cf. 33:11).'[8] From God alone, then, is there consolation, help and deliverance. Death can never be a consolation in and of itself, nor can death be considered to have meaning even when considered as a judgement of God. For God Himself is not ambivalent: He desires life, and not death and therefore death is never considered as having meaning or significance in itself. The Hebrews never attempted to find significance in death itself, either as a psychological experience or as a theological theme.

The Old Testament does not view death as an ontological

necessity, says Otto Weber, but rather as an intervention made by God. The Old Testament does not know of an independent power of death, hypostatized as the opponent of God. 'The actual power of death is the power of God in his concealment.'[9] It is not death we are to fear, but God who is the Lord of death even as He is the Lord of life.

While there is a theme of immortality as a promise to human persons in Israel's theology, this is often vague and related to the promise of having sons as a guarantee of a future posterity. One can see this quite explicitly in the covenant promise to Abraham, for example (Genesis 12:1–3; 15:1–6). This theme of immortality is not always connected to the theme of resurrection from the dead. In fact, the concept of resurrection as redemption from death is at best only dimly perceived.

If there can be said to be an expectation of redemption from death, it is only hinted at, and it is solely an expectation based on the promise and power of God not to forget those whom He has elected to be His own. Even the few passages which seem to speak of this redemption do not seem to promise resurrection from the dead for the individual (cf. Psalms 16:10; 17:15; 27:13). Psalm 49:15 appears stronger when it says: 'But God will ransom my soul from the power of Sheol, for he will receive me.' But, as Karl Barth points out, 'This does not seem to mean any more than that the man who trusts in God, in contrast to those who put their trust in power and riches, has no need to fear these two enemies and the consequent threat of death.'[10] The Psalmist does not express fear of death, but fear of the power of those who use power and riches to threaten his life (cf. vv. 5–9, 16ff).

Even the startling passage in Job 19:25 does not directly speak of resurrection in the sense of life beyond death. 'For I know that my Redeemer lives, and at last he shall stand upon the earth; and after my skin has been destroyed, then from my flesh I shall see God, whom I shall see on my side.' At most, this passage affirms that God will be his advocate and the source of his life *on earth*. It does not look to continuation of life apart from some form of continued earthly existence.

We seem to be on much stronger ground with the quite explicit statement in Daniel 12:2: 'And many of those who sleep in the dust of the earth shall awake, some to everlasting life, and some to shame and everlasting contempt.' Here we have the clearest statement in the Old Testament as to a possible resurrection from the dead, though what the precise form of this life after death is, we are not told. Some have argued that this rather late tradition in the Old Testament actually has its origins in the influence of the Zoroastrian beliefs about immortality upon the Hebrews through their exposure to these views during the period of the Babylonian captivity.[11] It is not within the scope of this discussion to render a decision on that matter. My purpose has been to point out that there is no clearly developed theology of death and the afterlife in the Old Testament.

The Old Testament's view of death can be summarized thus:

1   The power of Jahweh extends beyond the power of death; death does not have its own power and is not autonomous as a force which can destroy the human person.

2   The human person still is an individual before God beyond death, and thus, is still connected to the community of the living, though as a shadowy form of existence with no vital power.

3   Death is a threat to both the body and the soul and, while there is no clear teaching on the immortality of the person as a natural right, there is the promise and expectation of immortality through God's promise; the hope of the dying is in God who has power to keep the life of the one who has died 'before Him.'

4   Death, therefore, has its greatest threat in depriving the person of life, which is a vital relationship to God, in which both body and soul are an integrated unity.

When we move to the New Testament, we find that the basic orientation towards death is in continuity with that of the Old. To be sure, the New Testament has before it the resurrection of Jesus from the dead as its basic eschatological theme, yet we find, to our surprise, that very little is said about death as a physical event in the New Testament. Helmut Thielicke even goes so far as to say that in the face of the triumph of Jesus Christ through resurrection, death itself has been 'marginalized' and given a lower status of a 'background extra on the stage of life'. We can even say, writes Thielicke, that there is something like a 'contempt for death' in the New Testament.[12]

In his helpful essay on 'New Testament Views of Death', Professor Leander Keck says that there is no such thing as a

New Testament 'doctrine of death'. He reminds us that when Jesus speaks of death he *assumes* death as physical reality and that he:

1   accepted without criticism the contemporary rabbinic categories of death drawn from apocalyptic thought, such as judgement, resurrection, reward, and punishment;
2   that he had no interest in disclosing the mysteries of death and what lies beyond;
3   and that death was not the central problem to be resolved, but rather it was one's openness to the Kingdom of God, from whence came the true blessing in life.[13]

Even the earliest Christian understanding of death, argues Keck, stands within this apocalyptic tradition, and merely modifies it. Resurrection was part of the whole drama of the end-time, which included judgement, the defeat of Satan, the vindication of God's pledge to Israel and punishment and reward. The resurrection of Jesus Christ, therefore, was not at first viewed as the basis for a new doctrine of immortality and resurrection of individual persons. Rather, if the resurrection of Jesus was true, then the age to come had already begun to dawn and this called for a new way of looking at the present. This did entail, as the apostle Paul made clear, the resurrection of individuals to eternal life as a consequence of the resurrection of Christ.

Because of this personal hope, Christians are to remain faithful under persecution, and even death, because their destiny has now been decided through God's action in raising Jesus from the dead. For the Apostle Paul, the resurrection of Jesus constituted the core of his gospel. The resurrection is directly related to the cross in this kerygma (cf. 1 Corinthians 2:2; 15:1–4; Romans 1:3; 3:21–26; 4:24, 25). Thus the resurrection of Christ has a soteriological rather than an anthropological significance as a major concern for Paul; it reveals God's purpose for salvation of the human, not the inner logic of human nature. Christ is the 'first fruits' of those who have died (fallen asleep), and as such, guarantees to all who belong to him that they too shall be raised – but each 'in his own order' (1 Corinthians 15:20–23).

For the New Testament, like the Old, the key issue is not each person's individual immortality, rather it is the fact that the universal fact of death has no power at all in the face of the living God. In the New Testament, this is the one who himself has 'died, and behold I am alive forever more, and I have the keys of death and Hades' (Revelation 1:18). The central issue is not whether man has an essence that survives death (natural immortality), but whether the God in whom he believes has the power and moral integrity to 'make good' with the life he himself has called into existence. This is eternal life shared in fellowship with God through resurrection of both body and soul. In the last analysis, Keck says, 'the central theological issue in the death of man is the character of God'.[14] I would make this stronger by suggesting that the central theological issue is the promise and power of God to give eternal life through resurrecting persons from the dead. This tells us that the character of human life is upheld, both in its natural state of being subject to death as well as in being saved from death.

The name of Jahweh, as the only source of consolation and hope in the Old Testament, is now revealed in the saving event whose subject is the man Jesus. It is Israel's God who has acted in the death and resurrection of Jesus. Thus, says Barth, 'The Saints of the Old Testament were not mistaken or disappointed in believing that the God of Israel was the Lord of the living and the dead, and in regarding Him even in death as their rock and refuge.'[15]

There will be much more to say about the resurrection of Christ and its implications for a Christian theology of death in a subsequent chapter. For now, it needs only to be pointed out that the general orientation of the New Testament is one which is in continuity with the Old with regard to these facts: that body and soul alike are subject to death; that there is no dualism between the immortal soul and the temporal body; and that the individual's hope for redemption from death lies in God alone, who is the Lord of both life and death rather than in personal immortality as an essential aspect of human existence.[16] The gift of immortality is the gift of eternal life with God experienced as a unity of body and soul through resurrection from the dead.

Thus far my purpose has been to show that, while the Bible has no clear teaching on death, it does take death seriously and provides a clear teaching as to God's promise and purpose to preserve human life through the experience of death.

It is now time to turn to some specific theological concerns in attempting to develop a theology of death. Remember that these concerns had to do with (1) the human person and death, (2) death as an aspect of human nature and (3) and what we believe about the immortality of the human self.

Our first theological concern can be stated as a thesis: the death of human persons is the death of a relationship between persons and God. Death is a threat to personhood, not merely a fact of natural life. For animals, death is a fact of natural life; this is not true for humans, who were created to share in a relation with God as their creator and Lord.

The doctrine of creation in Christian theology includes the belief that human individuals bear the image and likeness of God. This is based on the creation story: 'Let us make man in our image, after our likeness; ... So God created man in his own image, in the image of God he created him; male and female he created them' (Genesis 1:26, 27).[17]

Yet, we are also told that 'the Lord God formed man of dust from the ground, and breathed into his nostrils the breath of life; and man became a living being' (Genesis 2:7). Following the transgression of Adam and Eve, God subjected them to a life which is in bondage to the earth from which they came, and reminded them that these conditions would continue 'till you return to the ground, for out of it you were taken; you are dust, and to dust you shall return' (Genesis 3:19). It should be carefully noted, however, that there is no curse placed directly upon the man and the woman. The serpent is cursed (3:14) and the ground is cursed (3:17), but not the human person. Nor is death here called a curse upon human life.

The word 'death' is only mentioned in the creation account with respect to humans. The first humans are placed in the garden with the strict command not to eat of the fruit of the tree of knowledge of good and evil. The consequence of violating this command is death: 'for in the day that you eat of it you shall die' (Genesis 2:17). It is not said of animals that they would die, nor did God say to the humans after the fall that they would die. They would return to the ground and to the dust from which they came.

What are we to make of this? We must remember that this creation account is a theological document with its primary focus on the relation of human persons to God and to each other. The fact of biological death, of animals as well as of human beings, is assumed as common knowledge. What cannot be known through empirical examination of the phenomena of life and death is what constitutes the unique value and the significance of human life given the fact that biological death appears to be common to both animals and humans. The creation account seeks to address this issue, not to provide an explanation for natural death.

It is significant, in my judgement, that the creation of both animals and the human persons is placed in the sixth day of creation. The seventh day, which is the Sabbath day of rest, belongs to God alone; it is not a day of creation, but a day which represents fulfilment. The uniqueness of the human person, therefore, is not portrayed by a separate day of creation from that of animals, but through a relation with God. Human beings are creatures of the sixth day which are summoned into a relationship with God which points to a fellowship and fulfilment symbolized by the seventh day.

The creation account is written after the Exodus from Egypt and the giving of the law of the Sabbath as the day which orientates the people of Israel to God as an eschatological fulfilment (Cf. Hebrews 3:7–4:13). There is no 'seventh' day which defines the destiny of the non-human creatures. For all creatures but the human, creaturely (finite) nature determines destiny. There is no way for creatures to escape being what their nature determines them to be. A creature's destiny is determined by a creaturely nature, and creaturely life itself becomes 'fate,' in the sense that whatever befalls the creature within its finite nature becomes its destiny. Nature, life, death and fate all are part of a cycle for non-human creatures.

In contrast to this, human individuals, though sharing with all other creatures a 'solidarity of the sixth day', are under a different determination. This is a determination to share in fellowship with God a destiny and life which transcends the mortal and finite conditions under which it is experienced. Or, to put it another way, human life experienced as personal relation with God does not share the same fate as the natural life of other creatures.

The nature of human personhood can thus be described as follows. Persons are biological creatures, subject to all of the conditions and consequences of a creaturely nature, but who have been given the gift of freedom to be for and with God, and to be for and with the other person. As biological creatures, human persons are part of the continuum of natural life and death. For the non-human creatures, this kind of existence is fatalistic and deterministic. There is no escape. But for human persons this biological nature is not fatalistic. For persons are orientated towards life with God and opened up to life with one another which is a mark of the image and likeness of God.

What we mean by *humanity*, experienced concretely as human personhood, cannot be determined out of the creaturely nature which we share with all other finite creatures. Humanity is not an abstract quality of creaturely life, but is the *personal* quality of creaturely life which is distinguished by relation to God and relation to the other.[18]

This distinction is very important when it comes to a theology of death for human persons. Biological, or physical death is a fact of nature, and thus becomes the fate of all creaturely beings who only have this form of biological life. Human persons, however, while necessarily having biological life in order to exist at all, do not share the same fate as other creatures. This is because human life is essentially human personhood experienced under the limitation and conditions of biological life.

The relation between human personhood and human biological nature is not a relation determined solely by the biological nature of persons. This is because God upholds the human person in a relation of knowledge, love, obedience and worship. In technical terms, we describe such a relation as contingent, or non-necessary. Human personhood is contingent upon the promise and power of God, and thus is free from the natural determinism and fate of biological nature.

For biological life, there is a cause and effect relation between life and death. The human person, on the other hand, while having a biological nature, is not totally determined by this biological nature and destiny (death). Being contingent upon the life and power of God, human persons are not absolutely subject to biological death as a fate. This principle of contingency opens up the way for us to explore what might be meant by a 'human death' as opposed to the death of non-human creatures.[19]

The biblical account of creation describes Adam and Eve as

created out of the dust of the ground, as were the animals. Yet, we are also told that God himself breathed into them the breath of life, and created them in His own image and likeness (Genesis 1:27; 2:7). We have described this same event in more theological and technical terms by saying that human personhood shares with animals a biological life and death, but that personhood itself is not subject to this biological death as a 'fate'.

A theology of death for human personhood must also then include the realistic aspect of death as that which belongs to one's natural life. This biological continuum of life and death, which includes a finite and mortal creaturely nature, is a limit which God established upon the human person's earthly existence. Yet this limit does not become fatal because God also promises to uphold the human person through that natural limit through a personal and spiritual relation with Himself.

This introduces another possibility of death, which is the consequence of sin. Adam and Eve are placed within the limits of their creaturely and mortal existence and warned concerning an act of disobedience to the divine command, 'in the day that you shall eat of it you shall die' (Genesis 2:17). This introduces the possibility of another kind of death, the death of the personal and spiritual relationship which Adam and Eve experience with God and with each other. With the death of this relationship, their biological nature, with its own death, will become their fate. Thus, though they did not immediately experience physical death upon their disobedience, they now live under 'sentence of death'.

This is why we now say that the experience of being mortal, of having a finite, creaturely nature, is natural to human persons, but that the 'death of that creaturely nature' is not the end of personhood. This 'boundary' of finiteness and creaturely mortality properly belongs to humans as created in the image of God. 'Is not finitude a part of human identity?', asks Helmut Thielicke, 'Do not individuals have a right to the death that is ordained for them?'[20]

The answer to the first question is clearly yes. Finitude is a part of human personhood, which entails mortality as a condition of life. The answer to the second question, however, is not so easy. Can we say that individuals have a 'right' to the

death 'ordained by God?' Death as the end of human personhood was not ordained by God, even though persons were
placed within the limit of biological life and death. God has
ordained life, not death for those created in His image.

Yet, we must be cautious here. For biological death does
belong to the human person as a part of his natural life. There
is a right to natural life and thus a right to natural death.
What Thielicke seems to be questioning is the right of society
to 'take away' from a dying person the right to die one's own
biological death in one's own time. Thielicke has earlier
asserted that the physiological experience of death cannot be
anything more than a 'sign or pointer' to what is now a
problem – the death of the person. But the death of the person
is a theological problem, not merely an anthropological one.
For it raises the question of the individual's relation to God as
well as to the structure of the community in which personhood
has been experienced.

What then does Christian theology believe concerning death
and human personhood?

The death that human persons die as a consequence of sin is
more than the result of biological death. The opposite of
biological death is biological life. This is the case for animals,
but not for the human person.

Human death is quite different from the death of animals,
even though it takes place through the same process. 'The
opposite of human dying (executed in the medium of biological
death),' says Thielicke, 'is life from God.'[21] That there should
be, for human persons, a biological death which may be termed
a 'good dying', is problematic to this understanding of human
personhood and death.[22] One's natural death as a biological
creature must be placed within a context of divine promise and
hope for the continuation of life for death itself to be robbed of
its power to destroy life. This promise and hope, of course, is
the content of a Christian theology of death.

This brings us to our second theological concern. It has been
shown that the nature of human personhood is to be understood as an essential orientation to God, who is the living One.
The foregoing discussion was concerned primarily with the
issue of human personhood as related to the finite and
creaturely conditions in which that personhood is experienced,
particularly with regard to the experience of death.

The second theological concern with regard to death and the human nature is an extension of the first. This concern, however, focuses more on the abstract question as to whether or not human *nature* as distinct from human *personhood* had some original potential for immortality which was lost in the fall.

In teaching a course on a theology of creation, it never fails that a student will ask: 'If death came as a consequence of sin, was there no corruption and decay in the world before Adam sinned? If Adam had not sinned, would he have lived forever?'

One answer to that is as follows. The original human *nature* of Adam before the fall was mortal and subject to the corruption and decay of all created forms of what we call the natural world. Sin did not cause human nature to become finite and mortal. The biological organism was given its own temporal and finite life-span in both the human and non-human natural form. Sin caused a separation between the human person and the life-sustaining promise and gift of immortality which issues from God alone. This is the death which entered into the human race as a consequence of sin, and it is to this death that natural death now points with its fatal finger.

This thesis will be developed to show how we can understand human nature as such to be mortal and finite in its original form, and yet to show the way in which sin has caused death to enter in as a threat to human personhood itself. We will review briefly some of the traditional views in the history of theology and then look more closely at the concerns of contemporary theology with regard to death and human nature.

The theological issue as to whether or not human nature possessed some form of 'natural immortality' before the fall of Adam, is one of considerable debate within the history of theology.[23]

Traditional Protestant theology, finding its roots in Augustine, and fortified by the thought of Calvin, has generally held that death was not a condition to which Adam was subject prior to the fall. In this view, death entered the human race only as a consequence of Adam's transgression. Though it was possible for Adam to sin, it was not possible for him to die. Both the Lutheran and Reformed tradition seem to follow versions of this tradition.

Augustine, in the fifth century, elaborating on the Apostle Paul's teaching that sin came into the world through one man, and death through sin (Romans 5:12), wrote: 'the first men were so created, that if they had not sinned, they would not have experienced any kind of death; but that, having become sinners, they were so punished with death, that whatsoever sprang from their stock should also be punished with the same death'.[24]

In the ensuing Pelagian controversy, the local council (held at Carthage in AD 418) found it necessary to pronounce against the idea that Adam was mortal from the start: 'If anyone should say that Adam the first man was created mortal so that, whether he sinned or not, he would have died physically, . . . let him be anathema' (DS 222/101).[25]

Anselm, in the eleventh century, followed somewhat the same line by teaching that man 'was so created as that he was not under the necessity of dying, . . .' and 'It follows, therefore, that had man never sinned, he never would have died.'[26] It is widely accepted that both Thomas Aquinas and John Calvin followed the same teaching. As a result, there is a more or less unbroken tradition from the fifth century through the Reformation which holds that the original human nature of Adam was not mortal in the same sense in which all creaturely being is mortal.[27]

It appears that the traditional Augustinian view which became dogma for the medieval Church and which was given renewed emphasis by the Reformers, concentrated more on resisting the Pelagian view that Adam's natural state was essentially the human state of all sinners. The concern was to prove that death was a consequence of sin and thus that all people are now sinners by nature. Not much thought was given to the consequence of this view in terms of what a pre-fallen, immortal human nature would have actually looked like. The idea that sin introduced corruption and decay into the natural world was not considered unbiblical, in light of Paul's discussion in Romans, chapter 8. There was no real concern for the anthropological question in light of the priority of the soteriological question.

Modern theology, on the other hand, has taken the anthropological question more seriously and, as a result, seems able to make more subtle distinctions between human nature as originally mortal and human death as the personal consequence of sin.

The nineteenth century theologian Friedrich Schleiermacher, for example, building upon the thought of another patristic theologian, Irenaeus, took a more congenial approach towards the view that Adam was originally created as an immature, mortal being, who was given the possibility of perfectability. In this view, human nature has within it the 'telos' or principle of maturity which can extend beyond the limitation of nature as mere creaturely being. This view seems more attractive to John Hick, for example, who suggests that 'the Augustinian type of theology in which death is held to be the wages of sin should be replaced by an Irenaean type of theology which sees our mortality in relation to a positive divine purpose of love '.[28]

The Dutch theologian P. J. van Leeuwen argues that 'man as he was created was, and was willed and intended to be, a mortal being. We must deny that death is something unnatural, a break in God's creation'.[29]

Paul Tillich agrees that man is and was naturally mortal. Sin does not produce death, says Tillich, but 'gives to death the power which is conquered only in participation with the eternal. The idea that the 'Fall' has physically changed the cellular or psychological structure of man (and nature?) is absurd and unbiblical.'[30] For some, like Tillich, who do not take the biblical account of the creation of Adam as historical, human nature is a product of the evolution of the biological species. Sin is not a biological event, but rather an existential paradox centred in the alienation of the human self from God experienced as lack of faith. The death spoken of in the Genesis account of creation and the fall, therefore, is an existential and theological reality, not the introduction of mortality into the human race. A theological distinction is thus made between physical death as natural and spiritual death as unnatural, and caused by sin.

Those who take the creation and fall more as a depiction of the historical origin of humanity, such as Millard Erickson, speak more cautiously of a pre-fallen human nature which is entirely mortal. Previous to his transgression, Erickson argues, Adam *could* die; as a consequence of his sin, he *would* die. Human nature as originally created, he states, thus was in a state of *conditional immortality*. 'Given the right conditions,' Erickson writes, 'he could have lived forever.'[31] Just what those 'conditions' were, he does not explain, except to speculate that before the fall Adam had a body that was susceptible to disease; after the fall there were diseases for him to contract. It must be said that this view is a significant modification of the more traditional view, but it still suffers from the problem of treating disease, for example, as the result of sin rather than as having a biological origin.

The Roman Catholic theologian Karl Rahner likewise follows the more traditional view, though also with certain modifications. Physical death cannot be seen as a consequence of sin, in his view. Adam was not under the *necessity* of dying; but without sin, he would have brought his personal life to consummation through a 'death' which would have been a 'pure, active self-affirmation, attaining a perfection of an embodied kind yet open to the world in its totality, the perfection we now look for as the final result of redemption, and as the eschatological miracle of the resurrection of the body'.

This is a death 'without dying', as Rahner describes it, and apparently marks a transition from a mortal state to a state of immortality as a supernatural event through the sheer power of God. Man thus, moves towards this natural end of life in death as a 'goal inwardly striven for', not merely as a consequence of nature.[32]

Karl Barth has given the most definitive answer to the question concerning death and human nature. Our finite being, argues Barth, belongs to our original God-given nature and is not the result of sin. Barth, in effect, makes a critical distinction between 'dying' and 'death'. The experience of dying is intrinsic to our created human nature. Human nature is not potentially orientated to immortality (Erickson), nor driven by some inner principle towards death as a 'final decision' which relates us to God (Rahner).

> This means that it also belongs to human nature, and is determined and ordered by God's good creation, and to that extent right and good, that man's being in time should be finite and man himself mortal. The fact that one day he shall have been answers to a law which does not inevitably mean that we

are imprisoned, fettered and condemned to negation by its validity. Death is not in itself the judgment. It is not in itself and as such the sign of God's judgment. It is so only *de facto.* Hence, it is not to be feared in itself, or necessarily, but only *de facto.*[33]

Barth can thus argue that dying can be held to be intrinsic to human nature as originally created by God. Whatever corruption and liability to death there is in nature, including disease, are present in the world before there is sin. Yet, this empirical reality of human nature has no absolute power over Adam, because he is upheld as a human person in his human nature by the sovereign power of God as creator and Lord of life and death.

This supports the answer to the student's question put earlier, and relieves us of having to postulate the somewhat grotesque notion of a pre-fallen human nature where none of the biological laws of decay and corruption as presently known apply.

Here we see the value of considering death and the human *person* as a theological theme before we look at death and human *nature.* When death is discussed in terms of human nature, there is an inherent problem created by considering both nature and death as an abstraction. What is missing in this approach is the contingent relation between human person and human nature as discussed above, in the first theological issue. When we confuse nature and person, death must mean the same thing for human persons as it does for human nature. In my view, however, the question of death must be dealt with only after a distinction between person and nature can be upheld. This allows us to accept the view that there is a death which belongs to human nature as such because human nature is biologically grounded. But this also permits us to interpret death as a consequence of sin in other than strictly physical terms. As will be shown, this also permit us to understand how this 'second death' can be removed as a threat against human personhood and yet human persons still be subject to biological death.

For all creatures but the human, dying is itself a natural 'fate'. The human person participates in dying through a human nature which is thoroughly finite and mortal. Death, as we have now defined it (personal and spiritual), in distinction from dying (natural and physical), strikes directly at the human person by threatening the person with loss of relation to God and to the community in which one's personal identity is bound up.

Having made this distinction, Barth is now able to take with full seriousness the fact of 'death' as an effect of sin and as a judgement of God upon the human person.

> In the judgement of God man is in fact a sinner and a debtor, and therefore by divine sentence subject to death, i.e. to death in the harsher sense, the 'second death.' And Jesus Christ has actually gone in our place to death, to death in this second sense, in this absolute negative sense of the term. . . We know the end of our temporal existence, our death, only as it is overshadowed by His death. Even though those who face death with their hope fixed on God. . . know that death is vanquished in virtue of the death which Jesus Christ has suffered in our place. . . The death which is behind them is an evil, an enemy of man. In the light of this fact there can be no doubt as to the unnatural and discordant character of death.[34]

It is this death which to the human person is an unrelenting evil, and which is concealed in our dying as a mortal human individual.

As a result of this distinction between the dying of human nature and the death of human persons, it may not be helpful to distinguish between physical death and spiritual death as a means of showing the effect of sin. But it is also true, as we have shown, that there is a personal and spiritual aspect to death as a consequence of sin. Sin affects the entire person, spiritually and physically. So too, the death of human persons as a consequence of sin affects one's spiritual orientation to God as well as one's physical orientation to creation. It would appear more helpful then, to distinguish between the dying of human nature and the death which threatens human persons, as we have attempted to do.

To summarize discussion of this second theological concern, we can say this. Humanity as originally created by God was not immortal, either actually or conditionally. Human persons, however, as created in the divine image and likeness, were under the summons of God to enter into the gift of immortality experienced as transformation of mortal human nature into the immortality which is actually achieved through the resurrection of Jesus from the dead (cf. 1 Corinthians 15:35–58). This position avoids the problems created by suggesting that there was originally a 'natural immortality,' or even a 'conditional immortality'. The view that there was an alteration of human nature by sin, or even the introduction of death-producing disease through sin, is not, in my judgement, a valid biblical interpretation.

To this point I have dealt with two theological concerns: (1) death and human personhood, and (2) death and human nature. The third theological concern that requires examination in the development of a theology of death has to do with a belief in the immortality of individual life in terms of survival after death.

The concept of the immortality of the soul, or of the immortality of the human self as a natural state, is not a concept that finds support in the Bible.

Man is not immortal, Otto Weber states flatly. 'Viewed from the biological structure of man, an 'immortal' being is unimaginable.'[35] This, of course, does not foreclose the possibility that the human person possesses an immortal soul, or self, which is more than biological life and therefore not subject to biological death.

The belief that human persons possess an immortal soul, however, runs contrary to the Hebrew anthropology which, as we have seen, defines the soul and body as both subject to death. There is no concept of an immortal soul in Hebrew anthropology as presented in the Old Testament.[36] The New Testament does not once mention the 'immortal soul:' the word 'immortal' occurs only three times, and then the immortality is not attributed to the soul but to the risen Christ and the embodied person in the new age (cf. 1 Corinthians 15:53ff; 1 Timothy 6:16).

Yet, there is within the Christian tradition a persistent teaching that the soul of human persons possesses some kind of immortality by nature. It has been widely accepted that the neo-platonic emphasis on a body–soul dualism, with immortality attributed to the soul, had significant influence in early patristic theology.[37] As a result, there existed in the medieval Church a strong belief in the immortality of the soul. The doctrine of the immortality of the soul was declared official dogma by the Lateran Council of 1512, and was accepted in principle by the Protestant Reformers.[38]

It should also be noted, however, that this tradition did not go unexamined. Thomas Aquinas rejected the older Greek view that the soul can reach its perfection through an immortality apart from the body: 'The soul united with the body is more like God than the soul separated from the body, because it possesses its nature more perfectly.'[39] This view of Thomas, of course, does not deny the immortality of the soul, but gives to the soul an Aristotelian capability of providing the body its final telos through resurrection. What this view did contribute to Christian doctrine was the concept of an intermediary state through which the soul could be 'purified' and so capable of experiencing the 'beautific vision' as a goal of its natural immortality. Thus, the doctrine of purgatory arose, referring to the state or place in which souls which will ultimately be united with their bodies experience this purification. The problem of time and the intermediate state which this view entails will be discussed in chapter 6.

The critical issue in the doctrine of the immortality of the soul is that of the continuity of the self through the dissolution of the body in death. In the biblical view, sketched above, this continuity resides in the continued power of God who created the human person in his own image and likeness, and who upholds that person in a relation which guarantees life, even in the face of being mortal by nature. This continuity of life beyond death in terms of the essential unity of body and soul is strongly supported by the biblical teaching on the nature of the resurrection of the body as well as the soul to eternal life.

The theological problem with theories of the immortality of the soul is that death is not taken seriously as a limit placed upon human persons as embodied souls and ensouled bodies. 'The passing of the sentence of mortality on the human race', says Thielicke, 'meant that a limit was set to the limitless. We were compelled to experience the fact that we are *only* human, *only* dust, and separated from God by an infinite qualitative distinction.'[40]

The concept of immortality as a quality of life intrinsic to human persons, however it is conceived, strikes at the heart of our authentic humanity. This was perceived correctly by the

8   *Church Dogmatics*, volume 3, part 2, pp. 616–17.

9   *Foundations of Dogmatics*, volume 1, (Grand Rapids: Eerdmans, 1981), p. 624.

10 *Church Dogmatics*, volume 3, part 2, p. 618.

11 John Hick, for example, *Death and Eternal Life*, pp. 70ff. For extended discussion of the Old Testament passages which seem to speak of life after death, see Karl Barth, *Church Dogmatics*, volume 3, part 2, pp. 618ff.

12 *Living With Death* (Grand Rapids, Eerdmans, 1983), p. 32.

13 In *Perspectives on Death*, pp. 35ff.

14 Ibid., p. 98.

15 *Church Dogmatics*, volume 3, part 2, p. 623.

16 This is not to ignore the fact that there are significant differences between the Old Testament and New Testament with regard to death and resurrection. E. Jüngel points out very perceptively that in contrast to the Old Testament (particularly the negative view of death as represented by, e.g. Isaiah 38:18ff.), the New Testament views death and life as both relativized by faith in Christ. As a result, one can glorify Christ 'whether by life or death' (cf. Philippians 1:20). However, this is precisely what Leander Keck has pointed to as the radically new perspective *on life* which results from the eschatological event of Christ's resurrection from the dead, and does not become the basis for a radically different view of death as belonging to the spectrum of human life. For the Old Testament as well, life and death are relative in relation to God, though the eschatological vision is only dimly perceived. See *Death: The Riddle and the Mystery*, p. 83.

17 For a discussion of the image and likeness of God as a basis for understanding human personhood, see Ray S. Anderson, 'Being Human – In the Image of God', in *On Being Human* (Grand Rapids: Eerdmans, 1982), pp. 69–87; 215–26.

18 For a discussion of the difference between humanity and creatureliness, see K. Barth, *Church Dogmatics*, volume 3, part 2, p. 249.

19 I have discussed the concept of contingency as it relates to human personhood in *On Being Human*, pp. 25ff.

20 *Being Human. . . Becoming Human*, (Garden City, NY: Doubleday, 1984), p. 87.

21 *Living With Death*, p. 34.

22 Cf. Otto Weber, *Foundations of Dogmatics*, volume 1, p. 627. Against this view, E. Jüngel argues, 'Set free from the curse of death, life's end may therefore be understood more precisely as man's *natural death*, as the end of that existence which he is by nature': *Death: The Riddle and the Mystery*, p. 92.

23 Richard Doss makes the claim that the issue of natural immortality is a 'watershed' in the history of Christian theology in *The Last Enemy* (New York: Harper and Row, 1974), p. 67. This is probably an overstatement.

24 *The City of God*, book 13, chapter 3.

25 Cited in *What a Modern Catholic Believes About Death*, by Robert Nowell (Chicago: Thomas Moore Press,1972), p. 14.

26 *Cur Deus Homo?*, book 2, chapter 2.

27 *Death and Eternal Life*, p. 208.

28 'Towards a Christian Theology of Death,' in *Dying, Death and Disposal*, edited by Gilbert Cope (London: SPCK, 1970), p. 25. See also: *Death and Eternal Life*, pp. 209ff.

29 Cited by G. C. Berkouwer, *Man: The Image of God* (Grand Rapids: Eerdmans, 1962), pp. 199ff.

30 *Systematic Theology*, volume 2 (Chicago: University of Chicago Press, 1957), pp. 66, 67.

31 *Christian Theology*, volume 2 (Grand Rapids: Baker Book House, 1984), p. 613.

32 *On the Theology of Death*, (New York: Herder and Herder, 1967), pp. 34, 37. E. Jüngel, however, disputes Rahner's thesis that death is a natural conclusion and a 'final decision' towards which man is orientated. Death as a phenomenon of human nature, counters Jüngel, is the end of existence which man is by nature. It has no teleological significance of its own through some kind of inner principle. *Death: The Riddle and the Mystery*, pp. 91-2.

33 *Church Dogmatics*, volume 3, part 2, p. 632.

34 Ibid., volume 3, part 2, p. 628. Cf. E. Jüngel who feels that the concept of 'second death' to which Barth refers is misleading and an unfortunate tendency carried over into contemporary theology from the Augustinian tradition. Jüngel fears that this emphasis on a spiritual death rather than a physical death undermines the seriousness of death itself as an event which the human person must experience: *Death: The Riddle and the Mystery*, pp. 92ff. For views that question Barth's distinction between natural dying and death, see Josef Pieper, *Death and Immortality* (New York: Herder and Herder, 1969), pp. 47ff. Oscar Cullman flatly calls death unnatural and even abnormal and, from the point of view of the New Testament, he says, he would 'not venture to join Karl Barth . . . in speaking of "death as natural".' Cited by Pieper, pp. 50-1.

35 *Foundations of Dogmatics*, volume 1, pp. 619-20.

36 See my essay, 'Body, Soul and Spirit', in *On Being Human*, pp. 207-14. See also, Hans Walter Wolff, *Anthropology of the Old Testament*, pp. 99ff.

37 See Josef Pieper, *Death and Immortality*, pp. 104ff.

38 Cited by Richard Doss, *The Last Enemy*, pp. 85–6.
39 Cited by J. Pieper, *Death and Immortality*, p. 41.
40 *Living with Death*, p. 157.
41 Cited by J. Choron, *Death and Western Thought*, pp. 135, 97.
42 Cited by K. Vaux, *Will to Live/Will to Die*, p. 56.

CHAPTER 4

Divine Judgement and Life After Death

As a small boy, I often worried more about what would happen to me after death than about dying. Where did this fear come from? From well meaning church school teachers, no doubt, who dramatically impressed upon me the picture of hell and eternal punishment which awaited those who did not please God in this life.

If there is life after death, it may be more of a threat to us than a comfort and consolation if, indeed, there is punishment in death and retribution following.

Halvard Solness, the master builder in Ibsen's play, admits that he is afraid to climb the scaffolding of a tower which he has built.

Hilda: Afraid of falling and killing yourself?
Solness: No, not that.
Hilda: What, then?
Solness: Afraid of retribution, Hilda.

Raised in a pious home, Solness worried that the structures which he built might be a tower of Babel, a symbol of his rivalry with God. 'I pretty well got the idea that He wasn't pleased with me.'[1]

Hamlet too worries about retribution after death, even as he ponders suicide as a welcome end to the slings and arrows of outrageous fortune:

> But that the dread of something after death,
> The undiscover'd country from whose bourn
> No traveller returns, puzzles the will,
> And makes us rather bear those ills we have
> Than fly to others that we know not of?
> Thus conscience does make cowards of us all . . .[2]

Perhaps Hamlet has studied the Bible too. Death as a form of punishment for sin would seem to be sufficient. That at least would be an escape from the distress of life and the presence of God. One could at least pay for one's sins through the act of dying.

But it is not that simple: 'It is appointed for men to die once, and after that comes judgement . . .' is the solemn pronouncement of the biblical author (Hebrews 9:27). To be sure, this is mitigated by the fact that theological reflection upon the death of Christ lead early Christians to believe that this judgement had already been borne by Christ. 'There is therefore no condemnation for those who are in Christ Jesus', sings the Apostle (Romans 8:1). But the hesitation remains. Can our faith really be so confident and secure that this threat is totally removed from our anxious hearts? The possibility of punishment for sins after death can be a crisis of faith for many people.

There is also a theological problem. If death itself is the 'wages of sin' (Romans 6:23), and if death is the punishment which falls upon the entire race (Romans 5:12–15), why would God hold out the threat of judgement against persons even after they have died? What is there about death that 'will not die', to recall Augustine's phrase?[3]

Before we focus more directly on the theological issue of punishment after death, it may be well to remind ourselves that fear of divine retribution following death is not a fear introduced into the human experience through the biblical literature alone.

In his important book *The Judgment of the Dead*, S. G. F. Brandon documents the fact that many cultures portray death as an evil which results from defilement of life, and even speak in lurid language about torment and judgement following death. Thus, not only in the New Testament, but also in the literature of ancient Egypt, Iran, India, China and Japan, under the influence of Hinduism and Buddhism, references to punishment after death are to be found.

While the representation of the joys of the just has generally tended to be of a rather symbolical kind, the sufferings of the damned have been depicted with such brutal realism that, except for a difference of artistic idiom, a medieval Christian picture of hell might well have portrayed Orphic, Muslim, Tibetan, Chinese or Japanese expectations of the fate of the damned.[4]

One thousand years before the time of Moses, inscriptions on the tombs of Egyptian kings reveal expectations of avoiding future punishment beyond death on the basis of good deeds performed during life.

Small boys in Egypt, too, went to sleep with visions of torment after death troubling them more than death itself!

The purpose of this chapter is to explore the theological meaning of the concept of punishment after death by developing four specific areas of the subject: (1) the development of the concept of punishment after death in the Bible; (2) what it means to say that Jesus Christ suffered God's judgement upon sin in his death; (3) the effect of Christ's death on behalf of sinners; and (4) some personal and pastoral implications of the issue.

Our concern, first of all, is what the biblical teaching is concerning death as punishment for sin and for judgement following death. 'Is thy steadfast love declared in the grave, or thy faithfulness in Abaddon? Are thy wonders known in the darkness, or thy saving help in the land of forgetfulness?' (Psalm 88:11). This is a fair question. Obviously, the Psalmist has in mind the separation from God which death seems to entail, but this does not mean that Jahweh's power does not reach into the kingdom of the dead or that even there anyone can hide from him (Psalms 139:8).

At least he *wants* to believe this as assurance against the unknown terrors that lie beyond death.

The Old Testament does not have a clearly developed theology of death as punishment. As noted earlier, the threat of death as a consequence of disobedience in the case of Adam does not distinguish between physical death and human death as separation from God. After the fall, death is not specifically mentioned as a 'curse;' rather, life itself comes under the burden of death as the ground is cursed and the dust from which man is taken is left to swallow him up again.

In the New Testament we face quite a different picture. Jesus certainly spoke of 'Gehenna' (hell) in depicting the afterlife.[5] To understand the context in which this language is used, one must remember the development of apocalyptic thought during the period between the Old and New Testaments. Apocalyptic, as used here, denotes a divine intervention of cosmic significance, usually portraying events which have to do with the end of the age and which involve events within history and beyond history having to do with the destiny of human beings.

In this literature a theory of rewards and punishments following death is depicted. The dead are no longer 'shadows' which exist in Sheol without form or personality. They are spoken of as souls or spirits and survive as individual conscious beings. Moral obligations appear in Sheol. There the good and the bad receive compensation for their deeds done on earth. In 1 Enoch 22:10–11, Sheol is a place of torment, though the actual word 'Gehenna' is not used. Whether the inhabitants of Sheol have a 'body' of some kind is not clear.[6]

Some feel that Jesus took over these ideas and expressed his own teaching in concepts and terminology borrowed from this literature. Certainly this would not be done without a great deal of selectivity and discrimination in his use of the concepts. What is even more important for us, is that it is quite clear that the early Christian community, which formulated a specific interpretation of the death and resurrection of Christ, drew upon this literature in giving substance and meaning to the eschatological content of Jesus' victory over death.

The appearance in later Judaism prior to the birth of Christ of quite specific views of the resurrection of the dead and personal immortality is generally quite well known. The Pharisees held these views as essential to their orthodox Judaism as contrasted with the Sadducees (cf. Matthew 22:23; cf. Acts 23:6–8). Jesus reflected the position of the Pharisees when he told the parable of the marriage feast, and spoke of the 'resurrection of the just' where those who have done well will receive their reward.[7]

This represents a significant development from the perspective of the Old Testament itself, though it can also be argued that this development is not outside of the inner logic of the Old Testament view of God as a God of holy, covenant love, who would not allow His people to perish at death. The urge to extend the jurisdiction of Jahweh over the abode of the dead was a perfectly natural development. The appearance in this literature of doctrines of resurrection, rewards and judgement, and even of a place of torment where those who resisted God continue to exist in their statement of rebellion, are not irrelevant addenda attached to a faith which did not need them. Rather, they were giving expression to the reality of God as the Holy One from whom no one can remain hid, and for whom darkness is as light (cf. Psalm 139:8–12).

In addition, we might say that the development of the ethical issues with respect to Israel's relation to God as seen, for example, in the writings of the later prophets, meant that death could not be detached from these moral issues (cf. Micah 6:6–16). The righteousness of God, so conceived in ethical terms, carried with it the theological cargo of consequences for actions done in this life. To allow death to annihilate the existence of the sinner, and so escape these consequences, would be to grant death a power over God's moral judgement. Thus, punishment of the wicked after death was a logical extension of the belief that the righteous would not be forgotten by a holy and just God.

The New Testament confirms and develops this theological development through an interpretation of the death and resurrection of Jesus Christ. While the kingdom of God has come in the person and work of Jesus, bringing judgement and decisive determination of good and evil with it, there remains an eschatological vision which includes a future judgement and decision. There the righteous will be rewarded and the wicked punished (cf. the parables of Jesus near the end of his life, Matthew 24–5; also, James 5:1–12; 2 Peter 2:4–10).

We have good reason to believe, then, that when Jesus and the early Christian community spoke of consequences of sin which extended through physical death and which warranted punishment and judgement in the life to come, this teaching rested upon a doctrine of God consistent with Israel's knowledge of Jahweh. These concepts were not invented out of their own imagination, nor borrowed from a literature which was alien to the Old Testament. Rather, the theological development of these concepts out of Israel's knowledge of God provided a language and conceptual pattern by which the substance of God's eschatological work in the resurrection of Jesus Christ could come to expression.

Some have mistakenly assumed that it is the Old Testament

which portrays death in negative terms, while the New Testament is positive and more 'human'. Actually, the reverse is true. It is the New Testament which fills out the contours of Sheol and populates it with people who have substance. Here we read of Dives, who in the realm of the dead is in 'anguish in this flame' (Luke 16:24). It is in the New Testament that we first hear of men being cast into outer darkness where they will 'weep and gnash their teeth' (Matthew 22:13). It is here too where we first read of the place where 'their worm does not die, and the fire is not quenched' (Mark 9:48). It is here that we read the terrible description of Revelation 14:11, 'And the smoke of their torment goes up for ever and ever; and they have no rest, day or night . . .'

Thus the reality of an afterlife is dramatically portrayed in apocalyptic language as the backdrop against which God intervenes through the extension of his own covenant faithfulness. Thus it is Jesus, the incarnate Son of God, who, as it were, peers into this cauldron of horror and shrinks from its terror.

Having surveyed the development of the concept of punishment after death in the biblical literature, let us turn to the theological question of what it means to say that Jesus Christ was judged by God on behalf of sinners in his death.

When the Apostle's Creed says of Jesus, 'And descended into hell,' it is faithful to the theological substance of the New Testament's witness to Jesus as one who took upon himself the curse of the law, becoming a curse for us (Galatians 3:13). As we have seen, the concept of hell as the abode of those who are guilty of breaking the divine law, is a clear theme in the New Testament. Jesus himself expresses a strong warning against allowing this to happen (Matthew 5:29; 18:9). It is God who is to be feared, and not man, because he has the power to 'cast into hell' (Luke 12:5). In becoming a curse and under God's judgement in his death, Jesus himself is placed in the condition of the sinner who is under the curse of the law.

On the basis of Christ's death for sinners, the Apostle Paul can argue that death, which spread to all people through the sin of Adam, has now been overcome through the death of the one man, Jesus Christ.

Therefore as sin came into the world through one man and

death through sin, and so death spread to all men because all men sinned ... For the judgement following one trespass brought condemnation, but the free gift following many trespasses brings justification. If, because of one man's trespass, death reigned through that one man, much more will those who receive the abundance of grace and the free gift of righteousness reign in life through the one man Jesus Christ. (Romans 5:12, 15, 16)

The death which Christ died, Paul continues, 'he died to sin, once for all ...' (Romans 5:10). The knowledge that the wages of sin is death, for Paul, is only known through the revelation of God. It is because Jesus died 'for sin' that he can say that there is now a connection between sin and death. Apart from Christ, no principle of causality can be drawn between death and sin, because both sin and death are related to God before they are related to each other.

The connection between death, sin and condemnation is entirely a Christological reality for Paul. He knows nothing of the power of sin apart from the reality of Christ. It is the law of the Spirit of life in Christ Jesus which has set Paul free from the law of sin and death. The law could not do this, because it was weakened by the flesh. But God has done what the law could not do, by 'sending his own Son in the likeness of sinful flesh and for sin, condemned sin in the flesh ...' (Romans 8:3).

For Paul, the statement that sin produces death is not an ontological statement with regard to a general principle of humanity, but it is a soteriological statement which points us to God's mighty eschatological work in saving us from sin and death. It is only after Paul knows by revelation (Galatians 1:11) that Christ has become the curse of the law (Galatians 3:13) that the connection between sin, death and punishment has been established. Christ, having taken the punishment of sin upon himself for all people, can now be viewed as the one man for whom that connection can be made absolutely. But this connection is now rooted in a saving act, not an act of condemnation. This is what is meant by saying that the connection is first of all soteriological rather than a a principle of general humanity. All people are now understood to be bracketed by the relation of Christ to Adam. In this relation, sin, death and punishment are now to be understood.

The fact that death is intimately connected with sin and

guilt is therefore a Christological statement rather than a general theological statement. It is only because of the 'free gift' which comes to all men through the death of Jesus Christ for sin, that sin, death and guilt can now be fused and accepted as a reality. But this reality is first of all a reality of divine grace and therefore has no power over us either as a future event or as an existential threat. We know this 'by faith', of course, but this faith is grounded in the objective reality of the free gift which has removed the threat once and for all; as a consequence we have 'peace with God.' (Romans 5:1)

Now we see that the solemn utterance, 'It is appointed for men to die once, and after that comes judgement,' is also a Christological statement. For it continues, 'so Christ, having been offered once to bear the sins of many, will appear a second time, not to deal with sin but to save those who are eagerly waiting for him.' (Hebrews 9:27–28)

It is now quite clear: the concept of punishment after death must be understood first of all as a statement about Jesus Christ and only then can it be related to other people. There is no depiction of the terror and torment of hell, there is no description of the wrath of God upon sinners, which does not fall upon Jesus Christ as the man who died and was brought under divine judgement on behalf of sinners. Here there is no need to soften or modify the strong statements in the New Testament concerning the wrath of God against sin and the terrible state of being separated from God.

'He descended into hell' say those who confess with the apostolic church. It is this death, it is this judgement of God upon the sinner, and it is this hell, and no other, that is spoken of in taking up the theological question of punishment after death.

But this then leads directly into the third area of discussion. Here the concern is with the effect of Christ's death and descent into hell on or for the human race. Is there a universal effect through Christ's death which exactly parallels the universal effect of Adam's sin? How do we understand the intent of Paul's argument when he says, 'Then as one man's trespass [Adam] led to condemnation for all men, so one man's act of righteousness [Christ] leads to acquittal and life for all men' (Romans 5:18)? Is the word 'all' extensive to the human race in both cases?

Some who answer yes hold that Christ's saving death has universal effect regardless of an act of repentance and faith on the part of individual persons. This is the position of those who might be termed universalists. Some who answer yes hold that Christ's saving death only contains a universal offer of salvation which must be appropriated through individual repentance and faith in Christ. This has been the more traditional view within orthodox Christian doctrine. Some would qualify the word 'all' in the second part of Paul's statement so that only those who are elected to salvation through God's eternal decree are included in Christ's saving death. Those not elected to salvation are considered to have been elected to reprobation, or eternal damnation, by a divine decree. This has been the view held by the more strict Calvinists in the Reformed tradition, usually known as the doctrine of limited atonement, or double predestination.

An examination of these positions lies outside the scope of this work. The central concern which these positions address, however, is one that we cannot ignore. This concern has to do with the concept of eternal punishment itself as a consequence of sin in light of God's character and his actions in Jesus Christ.

Brief mention of two arguments against the concept of eternal punishment following death will be followed by consideration of an argument from the traditional position which asserts that such a concept is necessary. An assessment will then be made in light of the previous Christological discussion of death and punishment.

There are some who argue on moral grounds that the concept of eternal punishment following death is inconsistent with a view of God who is essentially good and loving.

Is it consistent with the character of God to attribute to Him a will to subject certain people to everlasting retributive punishment? Dr Ian Ramsey thinks it is not, and has made a powerful argument against this idea.[8] The God of Jesus Christ, the argument goes, is a God of forgiveness and reconciliation. In Jesus Christ, God has shown His ultimate intention towards human beings as one of eternal love, not eternal wrath. The basis for this argument against the concept of eternal punishment appears to be based on a concept of God Himself, rather than upon some theory of the atonement. What is at stake is the character of God.

Others have taken a more existential approach to the issue of punishment after death. Paul Tillich, for example, interprets the biblical statements which speak of punishment after death and 'everlasting torment' as symbolic of existential despair and meaninglessness. The concept of 'eternal condemnation,' says Tillich, is theologically untenable, because God alone is eternal. Likewise, 'eternal death' cannot mean everlasting death, he argues, because death has no duration. The experience of separation from one's eternity is the state of despair (hell). 'Man is not cut off from the ground of being, not even in the state of condemnation.'[9] In this view, the concept of duration of time after death as expressed in the biblical language is taken to be symbolic, or mythical. But this position, as we shall see in chapter 6, redefines immortality and eternal life in the same way. As a consequence, eternal life is no more a state of being than eternal condemnation, except as a present form of existential reality.

There is, thus, both a moral argument and an existential argument against the concept of punishment following death, especially as eternal torment and these arguments can appear quite convincing to the contemporary mind. Is the only alternative a restatement of the traditional view that interprets the biblical language literally? Sin causes death, not only as a physical end of life, but in a spiritual sense, so that following physical death the sinner continues to pay for his sin through everlasting torment. Is this the doctrine on which orthodox theology rests its case?

Robert Morey thinks so. Sin caused separation from God (spiritual death) as an immediate effect, he argues. Consequently, physical death forces this separation into the state of disembodied, conscious existence, either awaiting judgement and damnation or resurrection to eternal life in fellowship with God. In this view, the effects of Christ's death and resurrection provide an eternal salvation for those who receive Christ by faith in this life. Those who do not, are not annihilated, but exist as conscious, personal beings in a state of perpetual torment (hell). As to the necessity of divine punishment after death, Morey says: 'We are convinced that the Scriptures clearly teach that God's character necessitates divine punishment and that He cannot simply pass over our sins and remain God at the same time.'[10]

Morey cites the Old Testament as well as Rabbinic literature to support the contention that God does hate sin and that 'everlasting' punishment awaits those who are not found righteous in his sight. Equally extensive are his citations from the New Testament as to this same general concept of eternal punishment. Morey presents his case as an apologetic for the traditional view that eternal punishment is a consequence of sin against modern trends towards a denial of personal immortality and universalism.

While allowing that the atonement made provision for the possible salvation of all, he insists that persons determine their own eternal destiny through a conscious decision for or against Christ prior to their death. Thus, physical death seals the fate of those who are already spiritually dead.

The logic of this is carried through relentlessly. With regard to those who have never heard of God's salvation provided freely in Christ, Morey insists that they will also suffer the punishment of hell. But because God is just, Morey says, 'there will be degrees of punishment in hell. All sinners in hell will be perfectly miserable but not equally miserable.'[11]

Just what this means, we are not told. It does seem to satisfy the sense of moral justice which Morey attributes to God as an abstract principle. Here too, we see that the character of God is at stake, but it is apparently a different God and a different character from the one known by Dr Ramsey.

Here we must make some assessment in light of our own discussion of sin, death and punishment as understood first of all as relating to Jesus Christ. The moral argument in favour of universalism and the theological argument of Morey against such a view do not appear to have developed the full Christological import of the New Testament's understanding of the death of Jesus Christ. What is missing from Morey's analysis is a Christological basis for interpreting this apocalyptic tradition in the Jewish and New Testament tradition. He appears to abstract the atonement from the history of Jesus Christ himself and make out of it an objective fact which needs to be appropriated through a subjective decision of repentance and faith before it has any effect at all. In the end, the justice of God is abstracted outside of the personal relation of Jesus as Son to the Father and outside of the ontological relation between Jesus and the 'all men' of Romans 5:18.

But here precisely is the problem of such a view, and the

reason why it remains unconvincing as a theology of death and eternal punishment. It is a theology which binds the freedom of God to principles of moral justice and speculates beyond the limits of what God has actually revealed through Jesus Christ. An alternative thesis can be stated in this way. We only know of the connection between sin, death and retribution after death in terms of Christ. This leaves us then with no basis on which we can speculate as to the status of persons who die 'as though Christ has not died for all'. Once Christ has uttered the cry of God-forsakenness, 'My God, my God, why hast thou forsaken me?' (Matthew 27:46), can we suppose that there will be those who will have to take this cry up on their own lips as though Christ has not uttered it for them? The Apostle Paul does not appear to think so. For if all have died through one man's sin, he has argued, 'much more' have all obtained the benefits of the 'free gift'. So he can conclude, 'in Christ God was reconciling the world to himself, not counting their trespasses against them' (2 Corinthians 5:19).

It appears that we are only permitted to speak of divine retribution as a judgement against the sinner in an absolute and 'eternal' sense when we speak of it as applying to Christ. To maintain a doctrine of retribution which stands outside of God's eschatological judgement upon death and sin is quite foreign to the New Testament. Karl Barth expresses the same idea with characteristic force:

> There is not a single eschatological statement even in the New Testament which allows us to ignore this One. His death, resurrection and coming again are the basis of absolutely everything that is to be said about man and his future, end and goal in God. If this gives way, everything collapses with it.[12]

Around this centre, says Barth, Christians consciously and the rest of humanity unconsciously stand somewhere on the periphery.[13] One's destiny is no longer determined by relation to death through sin, but through relation to Jesus Christ through faith. Christians, along with those who know nothing of Jesus Christ, are brought into the judgement of God which took place upon sin in this event. The connection which appeared to link death to sin is now broken. Death now relates all human persons to the living God, who is the God who has judged sin in His Son, Jesus Christ.

This is why, says Barth, speculation as to the status of those who die outside of knowledge and faith in Christ is forbidden to us. This is why talk of retribution after death can only take place with respect to this centre where Christ has taken this retribution upon himself, along with all of the implications of the terrible apocalyptic language of the New Testament, once and for all, absolutely.

Barth may have pointed the way towards a better theology of eternal punishment when he insisted that God has taken this punishment upon Himself, not merely as an abstract possibility, but as a concrete, real, human and absolute experience through His own Son. This, according to Barth, is the good news of the gospel which brings all people under the judgement of God upon His own Son through his death for sin and to make an end of death.

We are confronted with God, in death, says Barth. This means that in physical death we are confronted with the living God. But this is not a God who stands aloof, Janus-faced, as it were, with a face of wrath contrasting with a face of love. This is not a God who provides atonement from sin as an abstract possibility, having fulfilled his sense of divine justice and leaving us to choose either His mercy or His wrath.

This God with whom we have to do in death is the God who has already revealed His wrath and His determination to punish sin through the death of His own Son. God is the one whom we really have to fear, not death. But, as Barth writes, 'how can we fear the gracious God without finding comfort in Him?'[14]

This is not a general truth, which can be abstracted from the concrete life and death of Jesus of Nazareth. This is why universalism as a concept is unacceptable to many. It is only true 'in him', in the union of God with the death of Christ, in the judgement of God upon the person of Christ, and in the power of God poured forth in the resurrection of Christ from the dead and from the abyss of 'everlasting punishment'.

Those passages in the New Testament which warn of God's judgement and which speak of the danger of being found outside of Christ, cannot be used to construct 'another gospel' which places human beings under a divine law which has not been fulfilled in Christ. Nor can one speculate beyond the judgement of God upon sin in Christ and argue for a *de facto* universal salvation which disregards the personal relationship to God through Christ by which we are related to God.

There is a danger here of proceeding on metaphysical, rather than theological grounds. The need to 'universalize' the objective event of death, judgement and resurrection of Christ in such a way that this event constitutes an abstract 'salvation' without regard to God's disposition of the matter within the event of Christ, is sheer metaphysical speculation. It is no different in kind from the sort of abstract reasoning that led scholastic Calvinism to postulate a divine decree of reprobation as well as a decree of salvation within the divine being, resulting in the theory of 'double predestination' and 'limited atonement'.

It is difficult to follow this kind of objectifying of God's being and work which abstracts away from the concrete reality of God Himself as existing eternally as Father, Son and Holy Spirit. The doctrine of eternal punishment has been decisively answered within the divine Trinity. It is the task of a theology of death to hold accountable to this central tenet of Christian faith all theories and questions which might arise. This includes the doctrine of universalism as well as that of limited atonement.

Christian doctrine can only interpret what it is given to us to be known through the revelation of God as Father, Son and Holy Spirit; it is in this way that we can say that sin and death are overcome. 'Death has already attained its goal, the goal set for it by God, which was the execution of the divine No – in the One whose obedience ... was obedience "unto death, even death on a cross" (Philippians 2:8)'.[17] To take death seriously means to understand death as the death which Jesus Christ experienced. And to take sin as the cause of death in its most radical sense, is to understand the death which Jesus Christ experienced as caused by sin, and not merely by his mortal nature. To take eternal punishment seriously, is to understand the divine No pronounced upon Jesus Christ as absolute and actual, not merely partially and potentially.

The New Testament is unwavering in its insistence upon viewing sin seriously and death as the wages of sin, with condemnation standing within death as confrontation with the living God. When this is presented abstractly, it is a concept of God before it is a concept of death and punishment. We have seen that this is unacceptable from the standpoint of a theology that takes seriously the death of Christ and the judgement of God upon him in that death as the basis for the confrontation in death of all people.

We have also seen that this abstract view of God as one who upholds a decree of eternal punishment as though Christ had not already experienced this for all sinners, is unacceptable from a moral and existential standpoint.

An alternative view which many find to be more acceptable is based upon a doctrine of God which is derived out of His actions as Father, Son and Holy Spirit. This view upholds the theological integrity of the language of the New Testament when it speaks of sin, death and condemnation. These concepts are not filtered through the moral sensibilities of the modern mind, nor are they existentially interpreted so as to break the semantic connection between the words and the reality denoted. The witness to Jesus Christ in the New Testament is a consistent witness to the radical new event which has occurred through his death and resurrection.

There may be a time to remain silent when it comes to questions that force us to speculate beyond the knowledge we have in Christ. In light of God's revelation of His intention to take his own wrath and judgement against sin upon Himself, do we really know about the final status of those who die and who are confronted with this God? We do not know of a God who dispenses eternal judgement who is not also the God who has taken this judgement upon Himself in Christ.

The theological issue concerning sin, death and punishment in the New Testament is primarily personal and pastoral. Here we are lead into the fourth and final section of this discussion. Death is a highly personal and deeply existential concern. Fear of dying and apprehension concerning eternal torment following death is a source of great anxiety for many, and a matter of great concern for those who give pastoral care to the dying and their survivors.

My concern here is to look at the apprehension which surrounds death itself as a time of crisis with respect to an individual's relation to God.

The notion that the point of death is absolutely decisive for the eternal destiny of individuals is a development of medieval theology, based upon the questionable assumption that at death the 'indestructible soul' is separated from the body and goes immediately into its eternal fate. This led to an emphasis on death, rather than upon life. Any life, no matter how careless or evil, could be redeemed by a 'good death'. That is, a death which was preceded by repentance, confession of sins and faith in the saving merits of Christ's atonement.[15]

This emphasis on 'death-bed conversions' has continued into the evangelical tradition with the result that the human decision at the point of dying is often invested with eternal significance. Not only might this be a caricature of the gospel, which tells us that it is God's decision for us in Christ which is determinative, but it gives death and anxiety over death an 'evangelistic leverage' over the lives of the dying.

'To create anxiety about death only in order to witness to Jesus Christ as Saviour from death,' says Jüngel, 'is to do thoroughly objectionable theological business with death.'[16] This is not to say that the dying person should not have the opportunity to hear and be assured of the fact that Jesus Christ has already died this death for sinners, and has received the punishment that sin warrants.

We would miss Jüngel's point entirely if we took his warning as reason *not* to speak of the good news of Christ's salvation from sin and death with those who are dying. It is the gross appeal to fear of death as a basis for pressing people to accept Christ that he has in mind. The therapeutic value of sound pastoral and Christian assurance of the grace of Christ when confronted by death is indisputable.

What is proclaimed, in life as well as in the process of dying, is not an appeal to human decision as the decisive element in determining one's destiny, but the reality of Jesus Christ as the source of life and hope. Consent to the truth of Christ's atonement for sin and victory over death is sought because it is edifying and good in its own right, not because the certainty of eternal torment is a greater truth.

Death, then, no longer has the power to plunge human beings into a destiny of their own making. This power has been nullified and the 'sting of death' has been removed. The means by which death has been nullified in its power to bring condemnation has not been achieved by appealing to a motive of love in God more worthy of praise than His wrath; rather, His wrath has been felt totally and unmediated in the midst of

His love. The love of God in Jesus Christ cannot be known without also coming near to the terrible judgement and condemnation of God on the cross.

This is the benchmark of a theology of death. It is the benchmark by which all theories of human death must be critically examined and by which all statements about eternal punishment must be tested. This includes theologies that deny such a possibility through a doctrine of universalism, as well as those that insist upon such punishment as that demanded by the justice of God. It is the benchmark by which all strategies of pastoral counsel and care for the dying must be exercised. The issue of God cannot be brought into the moment of death without bringing the reality of Christ. Here there is an objective basis for forgiveness, healing, and freedom from fear.

There was no vision of Christ in the dark and threatening picture of eternal punishment that I, as a small boy, carried to my bed. There are some who will be sure that it was this threat of unending torment which drove that small boy to accept the 'solution' which Christ provides. But they will be wrong for Christ came on his own terms, from his own death, bringing healing and in peace. Easter is surely the proper perspective from which to look at the cross.

NOTES

1 Cited by Merold Westphal, *God, Guilt, and Death* (Bloomington, Ind: Indiana University Press, 1984), p. 119.
2 *Hamlet*, III.i.
3 *City of God*, book 13, 2, 11.
4 *The Judgment of the Dead: The Idea of Life After Death in the Major Religions* (New York: Charles Scribner, 1967).
5 For a scholarly discussion of the New Testament words Sheol, Hades and Gehenna, see *Death and the Afterlife*, by Robert A. Morey (Minneapolis: Bethany House, 1984), pp. 72ff.
6 For a discussion of this literature, see *The Method and Message of Jewish Apocalyptic*, by D. Russell (London: SCM, 1964).
7 For a helpful discussion of these issues in Jewish apocalyptic literature, see *Death in the Secular City*, by Russell Aldwinckle (Grand Rapids, Eerdmans, 1972), pp. 107ff; and George Ladd, 'The Resurrection in Judaism,' in *I Believe in the Resurrection of Jesus* (Grand Rapids: Eerdmans, 1975), pp. 44–59.
8 'Hell', in *Talk of God*. Royal Institute of Philosophy Lectures, volume ii, 1967 (New York: St Martin's Press, 1969), pp. 223ff.
9 *Systematic Theology* (Chicago: University of Chicago Press, 1957), volume 2, p. 78.
10 *Death and the Afterlife*, p. 103.
11 Ibid., p. 250. Dale Moody, in *The Word of Truth – A Summary of Christian Doctrine based on Biblical Revelation* (Grand Rapids: Eerdmans, 1981), holds a view quite similar to Morey on the resurrection of judgement and eternal torment (pp. 511ff). He too does not consider the implications of the judgement experienced by Christ as a judgement experienced once and for all, for all people.
12 *Church Dogmatics* (Edinburgh: T & T Clark, 1960), volume 3, part 2, pp. 623–4.
13 Ibid., p. 605.
14 Ibid., p. 610.
15 See John Hick, *Death and Eternal Life* (San Francisco: Harper and Row, 1976), p. 196.
16 *Death: The Riddle and the Mystery* (Philadelphia: Westminster Press, 1974), p. 131.
17 Otto Weber, *Foundations of Dogmatics* (Grand Rapids: Eerdmans, 1981), volume 1, p. 626.

CHAPTER 5

Christ's Victory Over Death

'I do believe that Jesus of Nazareth lived and died,' a student confessed to me.'I even believe that he rose from the dead. For that is a testimony to an event which once occurred. But can you tell me,' she continued, 'how I am to understand that his death and resurrection changes in any way my death?' The question is a fair one.

Central to the Christian faith is the belief that death has been destroyed through the death and resurrection of Jesus Christ; not just death in general, but the death of every person who 'belongs' to Christ through saving faith. Paul makes this claim central to his gospel, which is a gospel of God's purpose and power, 'manifested through the appearing of our Saviour Christ Jesus, who abolished death and brought life and immortality to light through the gospel' (2 Timothy 1:10). This is what Christian theology believes.

But in the New Testament so did Mary and Martha believe in the resurrection of the dead at the end of the age. None the less, their attitudes and actions concerning their brother, Lazarus, who had died, spoke more loudly about their belief in death than in resurrection. When Jesus told Mary, 'Your brother will rise again', she replied, as if reciting a creedal statement, 'I know that he will rise again in the resurrection at the last day' (John 11:23, 24). 'I am the resurrection and the life . . .' Jesus answered; 'Do you believe this?' Again, she replied in correct liturgical and theological form, 'I believe that you are the Christ, the Son of God, he who is coming into the world' (11:26, 27). So she passed her theological examination!

But the issue concerned a dead man, who had already been buried in accordance with what was believed about the reality of death. The stone placed before the tomb of the dead brother was not only to protect the body of the dead, but for the sake of the living, to anchor the emotions as well as the mind on a concrete point of reality. The technique of service to the dead comes with the practised necessity of survival in a world that is falling into chaos before our eyes.

'Take away the stone,' demanded Jesus in the story of Lazarus, and here faith faltered in the face of common sense. The sisters protested, and sought to discourage Jesus from any intervention into what they considered to be the way things were and the way things must be.

The situation Jesus faced here was not very much different from that which I experienced with my student. 'I am the resurrection and the life', Jesus offered, as a basis for Mary to connect a general belief in resurrection with the death of her brother. But she could not make the connection. While consenting to the fact that Jesus was indeed the Messiah, the one who was sent from God, Mary saw death in exactly the same terms as she had always seen it.

We see the same situation at the death of Jesus. Despite the fact that Lazarus did indeed come out of the tomb, and was presumably still alive at the time of Jesus' death, the death of Jesus was marked by a stone at the opening of his tomb. Those women who came to the tomb on the first day of the week were there to perform technical ministrations to the dead, not to witness a resurrection.

Indeed, the expressed concern was that the body had in fact been stolen. Mary Magdalene was not at all impressed with the sight of two angels sitting on the place where the body had lain. Turning to one whom she supposed to be the caretaker, she demanded to know where the body had been taken, so that she could recover it and perform the necessary and appropriate rituals which are for the sake of the living as much as for the dead (John 20:1–15).

If we permit it, our attempts to 'theologize' death will lead us directly to this impasse – the stones we place over the tombs of our dead will make unconvincing our belief that death has been destroyed. The fact that the legal stipulations for the disposal of the dead are often accompanied by a religious 'order for the burial of the dead', gives Christian faith a liturgical outlet for its expression of hope. But the face of death betrays no flicker of response. When the music has died out, the prayers have been offered and the last words have been said, the dead are surrendered to those who fill the grave and 'place the stone'. Then it is true, as Jesus said, 'the dead are left to bury the dead'.

My student's question has highlighted the central concern of this chapter: that is, to show how the resurrection of Jesus Christ can be understood as the redemption of the time and history of humanity through his own life, death and resurrection. In this way, we will then be able to show how his resurrection can effect the time and history of our own life. The resurrection of Jesus must be understood within the continuum of his own time and history and not in abstraction from it. Only then can we understand how we are given a place in his Easter history so that our life and death can be changed.

First of all, we need to examine more closely the context in which the early Christian community understood the significance of the resurrection of Christ with respect to the death of Christians.

The proclamation of the death and resurrection of Christ was the core element in the Apostle Paul's gospel. Beside the oral tradition which remembered the events of Jesus' life and death, which had not yet been placed in written form, the early preaching of Paul created a theology of a new order. In Christ, Paul argued, the old order, with its principalities and powers, had been displaced. Every aspect of life, including the power of sin and death, had been overturned by the resurrection of Christ.

The Churches which were formed around this eschatological vision were led to expect that a cosmic intervention had occurred through God's resurrection of His Son (cf. e.g. Romans chapter 8). In what is perhaps the first letter to one of these Churches, Paul had to write and give assurance in the face of the death of some of their own number. 'But we would not have you ignorant, brethren, concerning those who are asleep, that you may not grieve as others do who have no hope' (1 Thessalonians 4:13). Quite clearly, the Church was disturbed over the death of Christians in light of the message that death had been destroyed through the resurrection of Christ.

One wonders about the content of the sermon preached at the death of the first Christian to die following the resurrection of Christ. Ananias and his wife, Sapphira, expired under unusual circumstances, attributed to lying to the Holy Spirit (Acts 5:1–11). Their deaths no doubt were explained theologically as a judgement of God precisely because of this spiritual apostasy.

Stephen, of course, is one of the first recorded deaths of a Christian. He died as a martyr at the hands of the religious authorities who charged him with blasphemy against God when he attributed divine Sonship to Jesus, whom they had crucified (Acts 7:54ff). And then James, the brother of John, one of the original disciples, was beheaded by Herod (Acts 12:1–2).

We know from these accounts that death was not long in coming to the early Christian community. Luke does not tell us how they interpreted these deaths in light of the resurrection of Jesus. The death of the first Christians no doubt raised anxiety among the early Christian community. At the very heart of the Christian faith is the claim that God has intervened in the world of death through the death and resurrection of this one man. We must remember, however, that this claim is the result of the theological reflection of Paul himself. The early Christian community was concerned primarily to be faithful witnesses to the messianic claim, that Jesus of Nazareth was indeed God's anointed, the Christ. Thus, to die as a faithful witness to this truth was not considered to be a theological problem and possibly not a crisis of faith.

It was Paul, however, who interpreted the death and resurrection of Christ in cosmic and eschatological terms, arguing that in the death of this one man, sin, as the cause of death, had been cancelled and that the 'sting of death' has thus been removed (1 Corinthians 15:56). This later theology of Paul has its roots in the early sermons preached on his first missionary journey. Paul, recorded by Luke, is first heard preaching in Antioch of Pisidia. He concludes his message by asserting that through the resurrection of Jesus from the dead, 'forgiveness of sins' is proclaimed, with consequent freedom from all that the law of Moses could not grant (Acts 13:38, 39). While there is no mention here of death itself being destroyed through this resurrection, the connection between the death and resurrection of Christ and forgiveness of sins has been made.

On a subsequent missionary journey, preaching at Athens, Paul concluded that God has fixed a day in which all people will be judged, and 'of this he has given assurance to all men by raising him from the dead' (Acts 17:31). It was, in fact, Paul's argument from the resurrection of Jesus to the resurrection of all men that caused such mockery and disputation among the Athenians (17:32).

There are grounds for concluding, therefore, that even the early preaching of Paul emphasized the connection between the death and resurrection of Christ and forgiveness of sins, and consequently, the overturning of death as the result of sin. But it was this very connection which raised the theological question which first surfaced at Thessalonica. If death has been destroyed through the resurrection of Jesus, why is not death then changed? Why do Christians continue to die and remain dead in the same manner as before?

Writing to the church at Thessalonica, Paul writes as one not unfamiliar with death, even the death of Christians. He has, no doubt, spoken words of Christian encouragement and hope at the death of Christians. But we must remember that the emergence of a theology of death came about originally precisely through this 'pastoral' reflection upon the meaning of death in light of the gospel of resurrection. When Paul tells the Christians at Thessalonica that, 'since we believe that Jesus died and rose again, even so, through Jesus, God will bring with him those who have fallen asleep', he is stating a theology of death for Christians (1 Thessalonians 4:14). Paul's teaching is that 'The dead in Christ rise first' and 'we who are alive' will be caught up to meet with them, to meet the Lord, 'and so we shall always be with the Lord' (4:16, 17).

Death continues as a physical event in the temporal lives of Christians. Paul has never disputed this fact, to our knowledge. But this experience of physical death no longer has power to separate the person from God nor can it be understood as a consequence of sin. Christians do die, but this death is qualitatively different from the death that occurs to those who do not belong to Christ. Those who die are even spoken of as having 'fallen asleep'. These are not merely dead, they are 'dead in Christ' (1 Thessalonians 4:16).

Yet we ask, and the question is a fair one, 'how does his resurrection from the dead affect my own death such that it changes it from one form of death into another?'

We cannot understand the connection between the resurrection of Christ and our individual death without first thinking through the implications of Christ's resurrection to his own life and death. If resurrection appears to stand 'outside' of the realm of space and time, then it will be outside of our own temporal existence as well. This is exactly the problem created when one attempts to understand the resurrection as merely a historical fact, rather than as an event within the history of Jesus of Nazareth, who is also the risen Christ.

We must look first of all, then, at the connection between the resurrection of Jesus and his own life and death. The New Testament witness to the resurrection of Jesus makes quite clear the fact that the resurrection of Jesus is not explained through a general belief in resurrection.

Paul Tillich seems to have missed this point when he argues that the disciples of Jesus created the 'symbol' of resurrection along the lines of later Judaism's belief in a general resurrection to explain the ignominious death of the Messiah. The 'idea of resurrection', says Tillich, was used to explain the mysterious sense of Christ's presence following his death.[1] This view has been criticized by George Ladd, among others, who has shown that the belief of later Judaism prior to the resurrection of Christ was in an eschatological event that would mark the end of the age, not an event that would occur within history.[2]

The same language used to speak of the resurrection of Jesus is used in the New Testament to speak of other events, such as miraculous healings and even the raising of Lazarus. However, there is no suggestion that the resurrection of Jesus was merely an eschatological 'sign'. Nor was it viewed as taking place outside of or beyond the historical continuum on which other events occur. It is itself an eschatological reality which occurs within the space–time continuum, and which merges with the continuum of the life/death of others. This is most noticeable in the remarkable period of 40 days following the resurrection of Jesus when he was present to the disciples prior to his ascension into heaven. Only if we choose wilfully to set aside the New Testament testimony to the post-resurrection appearances to the disciples, and the period of 40 days cited by Luke (Acts 1:3–4), can we ignore this time and history of Jesus as coincidental with 'their' time. As it is recorded, these are not merely sporadic resurrection appearances, but 'while staying with them he charged them not to depart from Jerusalem. . .'.

While not limited to the same boundaries as his pre-resurrection existence, Jesus, none the less moved freely within these boundaries, not as a ghost, nor as a phenomenon of psychic experience, but in his personal presence as the Lord of this community of believers. The attempts to explain this testimony to the presence of Jesus among them on the basis of natural laws alone will fall short. This is because we are confronted with a reality of time and space through his resurrected presence that cannot be validated on the terms of the old history of death.

Here there is no dualism between the two levels of time and history, with a mythical connection created between the two levels. Nor can we extrapolate out of the former time and history to the 'Easter' time and history so as to explain the new out of the old. We cannot 'correct' the reports of the disciples concerning the presence of Jesus with them after his resurrection, as though we could bring their experience into conformity with a critical/historical viewpoint based upon the history of death. This approach confuses logical sequences of thought with temporal and causal sequences of events. The reality of the resurrection cannot be established by projecting a logic of the history of death into the reality of new life.

Exactly the opposite takes place. During these 40 days, their encounter with Jesus 'corrected' their understanding of his history with them prior to the resurrection. As T. F. Torrance has helpfully pointed out in his book *Space, Time and Resurrection*, 'The resurrection imposes upon all that has taken place hitherto an entirely different aspect, so that things begin to fall into place and steadily to take on a depth of meaning and consistency impossible to conceive before.'[3] This procedure is reflected in the attempt of Jesus to convince the two disciples on the road to Emmaus following his resurrection of the 'inner necessity' of the events of crucifixion and resurrection already present in the previous history. 'Was it not necessary that the Christ should suffer these things and enter into his glory?' (Luke 24:27).

This 'inner connection' between Easter time and history and the previous history of death can only be explained in terms of time and space itself being contingent upon the order of new creation, towards which it is orientated. The contingent relation is a relation which permits no dualism, but it is a relation which can only ultimately be explained and known out of the new creation.[4] There is a real correspondence between the person of Christ who is resurrected from the dead and the Jesus whom the disciples knew prior to his death. The New Testament witness goes to great lengths to establish this fact. But the interpretation of the history of Jesus with his disciples must now come from the resurrected Christ himself (cf. Luke 24). Their understanding of this correspondence and continuity is contingent upon his presence and communication with them.

Also, the appearance of the new creation through the resurrection does not destroy the natural order of time and space. The time and history of the disciples continues to take place within its limitations – it is still a history of death. Yet, this history has now been radically re-orientated to the new creation which already has impinged upon the old. The ascension of Jesus does not cause the former time and history to slip back into its time of death, but releases the truth of the new creation to be proclaimed through the message of Jesus as not only the Messiah of Israel, but as the Lord of all creation.

Thus we see that the connection between the resurrection of Christ and his own death is made within the temporal/historical continuum, but understood from the perspective of Easter history. Three things need to be pointed out in this regard.

First, the resurrection of Jesus was part of the unbroken continuum which is constituted by his birth, life and death. Thus, Jesus can say 'I am the resurrection and the life' even while he himself is facing his own human death. The 'I am' encompasses the entirety of his personal being, reaching from his birth (the assumption of human mortal flesh) to his resurrection and ascension in bodily form.

The resurrection of Christ has an 'inner connection' with his birth, and thus the entire reality of incarnation, says T. F. Torrance.[5] We are not to view the resurrection as some kind of 'timeless' event, or as a mathematical point which exists only tangentially with respect to our space–time existence. 'It would be quite unintelligible and nonsensical,' argues Torrance, 'if the consummation of God's work in space and time were not of the same tissue as all of the rest of it.'[6]

Secondly, the death from which Jesus was raised was his

own death, assumed through his birth, not merely death as an abstract concept. Karl Rahner insists that we must understand the death of Jesus in this way. 'As Christ became man of the fallen race of Adam, and assumed the 'flesh of sin', he entered human life in a situation in which that life reaches its fulfilment only by passing through death in all its obscurity.'[7] We remember that Rahner considers death to be the necessary fulfilment of human life, and as such Jesus has taken this death upon himself as well in becoming human. However, Rahner also holds that at death, the human soul is opened up to the cosmos as a whole. For man as sinner, Rahner suggests, this is loss of individuality and personality, and it is this death from which one needs to be redeemed. The death of Christ, then, in Rahner's view, inserts the life of God into the very ontological foundations of the cosmos, thus redeeming 'death' for all persons through this one death.[8]

'It is only because we have already become immortal in our lives,' ways Rahner writing elsewhere, 'that death and its threatening and impenetrable appearance of annihilation is so deathly for us.'[9] Does Rahner then believe that Christ's redemptive act was accomplished solely in his death, and not also in his resurrection? Probably not, for Rahner also says quite clearly that the concrete person reaches fulfilment beyond death '. . . as the finality of his personal history and as the finality of his corporeal and collective reality as a concrete person, that is, it can be expressed as the beatitude of the soul and as the resurrection of the flesh.'[10] It must be said, however, that the resurrection of Christ is not seen as the creative basis for human immortality in Rahner's thought, even though it is that which preserves the immortal life of the individual.

The concern in this discussion is to argue that there is an inner connection between the resurrection of Christ and his own death, which is the death which properly belonged to him through his assumption of humanity at birth. The fact that this death also entailed the death of a 'sinner' is, I believe, not merely a forensic decision rendered concerning this death, but also a reality connected with his real humanity. The very flesh he assumed is a human existence under 'sentence of death' due to the sin of Adam.

Thirdly, it must be seen that time as a constituent of human life is not annihilated in the resurrection of Christ, but re-created, as it were. Time is redeemed through the resurrection of Christ, not in some abstract sense, but *his* time is redeemed, and consequently, ours as well. The entire event of the birth, life and death of Jesus of Nazareth is re-constituted through resurrection in such a way that the continuum of created time and space on which human persons exist has itself been opened up to include this reality. The resurrection of Jesus, says Torrance, may be viewed as the 'humanizing in Jesus of dehumanized man, the establishing of the fact that man *is* – the end of all illusion, and all existentialist philosophies of nothingness'.[11]

This means, Torrance continues, the taking up of *human time* into God. With the ascension of Christ, this new creation is hidden from us in such a way that we relate to it through faith, and not by sight. None the less, it remains valid that in the risen Christ our human nature in its temporal and historical dimension is now also redeemed from the power of death to separate us from that reality.[12]

The argument here is that the connection between the resurrection of Jesus and his own birth, life and death provides the key to understanding how his resurrection can be connected with our time and place – that is, with our death.

This discussion centres on a concept of 'time', which includes the concepts of human history and temporality. Karl Barth, more than any other contemporary theologian, has no doubt offered the most profound analysis of 'time' in relation to the incarnation and resurrection of Christ.[13]

The New Testament does not encourage us to think that Jesus 'escaped' historical time, along with the limiting reality of embodied existence within time, says Barth. Rather, in his resurrection, Jesus is viewed as 'resuming and completing' his redeeming work begun through his incarnation. He is revealed through his resurrection to be 'Lord of the cosmos (time)' as well as 'Lord of the community'. Easter time, says Barth, is the same *time and history* as is birth and crucifixion (pp. 442ff). Resurrection is not an eschatological sign of a reality which stands outside of our time, but it is an event which redeems the time of Christ from the nothingness of death and its power to alienate the life of the flesh from the creator.

The problem of the resurrection and time is first of all an anthropological problem, says Barth (p.439). It is the problem of the existence of 'man' as a temporal, finite and historical being. For a human person to exist in a time that has come under 'he threat of death is to lose an essential aspect of humanity itself. The man Jesus has his 'life time' on a continuum of birth on the one end, and his human death on the other. If we abstract from this human 'life span' of Jesus, says Barth, we lose contact with the man Jesus entirely, and his resurrection will then be a meaningless and empty symbol (p. 440).

As it is, the New Testament testimony is unanimous in certifying that the resurrected one who appeared to his disciples and who moved among them for 40 days after his resurrection was the same man they had known in the flesh. What we must see, Barth argues, is that there is an inner connection between the Jesus of Nazareth who became known as the Christ and the Christ of the resurrection who enabled them to know Jesus of Nazareth as the one who brought them eternal life (1 John 1:1–2). The Easter history, concludes Barth, is the starting point for their history of Jesus of Nazareth so that death is no longer the arbitrator of his time (pp. 442–3).

In order for Jesus to overcome death through resurrection, he had to be 'able to die'. In order for God, as the eternal Son, to redeem humanity from death, he had to become human and so to 'share in flesh and blood' so that 'through death he might destroy him who has the power of death, that is the devil, and deliver all those who through fear of death were subject to lifelong bondage' (Hebrews 2:14–15).

Jesus overcame death, not by avoiding it, or transcending it, but by extending human time and history *through* death. This was done in the sphere of time and space, so that death itself is not removed, but time is transformed in such a way that it extends through physical death into resurrection.

This is a crucial point and it must not elude us. The biblical language to the effect that Jesus has 'abolished death' can easily be misunderstood (cf. 2 Timothy 1:10). The author of the epistle to the Hebrews says that 'through death he might destroy him who has the power of death, that is, the devil' (2:14). The resurrection of Jesus abolished the hold that death had on his life, and established his life beyond death as an essential continuation of his personal being and existence as

Jesus of Nazareth. Death continues to take place on this continuum, just as birth does. What has been radically altered is the power of death to end the personal time and history of human persons. This is what took place through the resurrection of Jesus as the 'first fruits' of all others who will be raised at his coming (1 Corinthians 15:23).

The enigmatic reality of our being in time is perverted and disturbed reality because our time is always human time under the sentence and contradiction of death. We cannot accommodate ourselves to this history of death and distorted reality of time. To accept death and the end of time as our 'fate' or to abstract from this time by spiritualizing our life is to place ourselves out of the time through which God is working out our salvation. Jesus was tempted to 'escape' the reality of death through exercising the prerogatives which belonged to him as a 'Son of God'.

This can be a temptation for us as well. We can be tempted to resign ourselves to death and accept it as the final reality of our life. Or, we might be tempted to spiritualize death in some mystical way, and so evade the human aspect of death, with its genuine sorrow and sadness. The death of other persons cannot be transcended through a spiritual or mystical perspective without also abandoning the person who is dying. The basis of all truly Christian ministry to the dying begins with seeing death as an event of that person's time and history.

Even as Jesus could only fulfil his 'time' through his 'obedience unto death' (Philippians 2:8), so we too fulfil our time through obedience and faithfulness – unto and through death. We are temporal beings, which means that our lives are bounded by the limits of birth and death. This is the reality of our existence as historical persons. This is true not merely in the sense of having had a history, but primarily in the sense of existing within the 'time' allotted to us by God. Our time and our history is contingent upon God's time and His history.

To say that God has a 'time and history' is to say that God's own existence is that of a relationship revealed to us as the relation of the Father, Son and Holy Spirit. This relationship within the very being of God has its own 'time and history', though obviously as uncreated time and history. In creation, God extended time and history through the finite dimensions of human personhood, contingent upon his own eternal 'time'.

Thus human time and history has its original limitation in the creative act of God, both as to its point of origin and its destiny.

Mortality, as an aspect of created nature, was not God's ultimate purpose for human personhood, nor was natural mortality the same as human finitude in this same sense. The human person is created as a finite being – this is one way of distinguishing between God and the human person. But as was shown earlier (chapter 3), finitude does not mean the same thing as mortality. Mortality is a condition which human persons have in common with all created things and beings.

Human persons by *nature* are mortal; human personhood itself is finite and not infinite being. The finite limits of the human person are determined by relation to God Himself, who is infinite in personal being. This allows us to say that the finite nature of human persons can extend beyond death. Our finitude will always be a distinction between our created being and God as uncreated being. Yet, this distinction has been taken up into the life of God through the union of the finite humanity of Jesus with his being as divine Son of God.

With sin, came loss of relationship to God, with the result that natural mortality now appeared to set the limit for finitude – this is human death. In assuming human nature at his conception and birth, the eternal Son of God re-created human finitude in its true 'image and likeness', and thus set the stage for destroying death as the power of mortality over the true finitude of human personhood (cf. Colossians 1:15–20). The resurrection of Jesus restored the time and history of Jesus of Nazareth by establishing his true identity as not being destroyed by mortality (death).

It was the experienced reality of this 'same Jesus' which gave substance and content to the idea of resurrection as victory over death. For this victory was not a metaphysical victory, but a physical victory in the realm of a physical death. 'See my hands and my feet, that it is I myself,' Jesus said to his disciples, 'handle me, and see; for a spirit has not flesh and bones as you see that I have' (Luke 24:39).

What troubled the Christians at Thessalonica was not a problem with connecting the resurrection of Jesus with death as a concept, but the perceived end of the time and history of their loved ones. Paul's assurance to them, therefore, did not have to do with an argument about the nature of death, but with the reality of the continued existence of those who had died and of the future 'time and history' of renewed fellowship with them. Until that time, Paul suggested, their time and history was hidden in the time and history of the resurrected Lord himself.

E. Jüngel, on the other hand, warns against attempting to use the resurrection as a concept which 'dissolves' life's temporal limitations. He argues that such a concept would involve the dissolution of human individuality. To 'infinitize' the 'I', he suggests, would mean that the temporal 'I' would no longer exist.[14]

However, upon closer examination, it does not appear that Jüngel is rejecting the concept of temporal existence being extended through death, as presented here. For his concern is that resurrection be understood to mean that 'the life man has lived' be saved, not that 'man is saved out of this life'. He also holds, as we have suggested, that our life is hidden in Christ's resurrected life. 'Our *person* will then be our *manifest history*' (p. 120).

Has this discussion helped the student whose question opened this chapter? I hope so. Let us summarize several points that have been made.

First of all, the question, 'How am I to understand that his resurrection in any way changes my death?', while it seemed a fair question, cannot be answered directly. The attempt to establish a connection directly between the resurrection of Christ as an object of belief with one's own individual death is impossible from the start. We have, thus, re-directed the question so as to focus first of all upon the connection between the resurrection of Jesus and his life and death. This places the question within a Christological rather than a metaphysical and abstract framework. Certainly there are metaphysical issues as well, such as questions relating to personal identity through the discontinuity of death and resurrection. But it is only as we 'think out of the inner connections' which belong to the time and history of Jesus himself that we can avoid setting up metaphysical and abstract problems for which there are no theological answers.

The discussion thus far has involved the following points:
1 The resurrection of Jesus took place as an event on the continuum of his birth, life and death.

2 There is an inner connection between the resurrection of Jesus of Nazareth and his death which belongs to the event of his own human, temporal life.

3 The resurrection of Jesus 'saved' him from death by extending his personal history through death.

4 Temporality, as a factor of Jesus' human personal identity, is thus redeemed from death by his resurrection.

5 By assuming a humanity which was limited by death, Jesus brought humanity within God's own time and history as the time and history of the eternal Son with the eternal Father.

6 Death has not been cancelled and replaced with something else; rather, the time of the human person as represented by Jesus of Nazareth has been extended through death, so that death no longer is the boundary of finiteness and the history of the human person.

This is first of all a theology of the death and resurrection of Jesus of Nazareth, but as such, it includes the death and resurrection of all persons who are united to this Jesus through a common humanity and through a shared experience in his resurrection life. This is why I have emphasized the inner connection between the resurrection of Jesus and his humanity as experienced in birth, life and death.

At this point there comes a transition in our discussion, to focus more directly upon how we might understand the resurrection of Jesus to have affected our life and death.

The incarnation has its basis in the life which is shared within the eternal Godhead, revealed to us through Jesus as the Son of the Father in the power and life of the Spirit. The fact that Jesus shares with us a common humanity is not itself enough to establish our participation in his resurrection. The principle of common humanity is easy enough to establish on the basis of life and death itself. We have no reason to doubt that death is a universal human phenomenon; we at least share that with all other humans. The fact that Jesus was human and that he died gives us reason to assume that we have a common humanity.

But we cannot argue from the principle of common humanity, because this immediately becomes an abstraction and the vital connection is lost. Each one of us dies 'his own death', despite our common humanity. And I suppose that if one of our fellow humans should suddenly reappear before our eyes in

what we would have to conclude is a resurrection from the
dead, we would be amazed and overjoyed, but not really
convinced that our own death would necessarily lead to this
happy ending.

This is what led my student to question the relation between
the resurrection of Jesus and her own death.

What I have attempted to show is that it is the inner
connection between the time and history of Jesus of Nazareth
with the time and history of God himself that is the core of
Easter faith. The resurrection of one or the other of the two
criminals who died upon the cross along with Jesus surely
would have been a source of amazement, not to mention
consternation. But there would be no basis for taking this as
any more than an exception to a general rule.

The resurrection of Jesus revealed the fact that he was
'descended from David according to the flesh and designated
Son of God in power according to the Spirit of holiness, . . .
Christ Jesus our Lord, . . . ' (Romans 1:3, 4). The inner
connection between Jesus of Nazareth and the life of God
Himself is revealed by the resurrection. This inner connection
is not an abstract way of explaining Jesus' relation to God.
Rather, the concrete relation of Father to Son and Son to
Father is the ground for the entire history of Jesus of
Nazareth, as a history of God with human persons, and human
persons with God.

For the Apostle, this means that the entire spectrum of
human life, from birth to death, has been radically reorien-
tated to this time and history of Jesus. It is not just that death
has been overcome and that there is now a 'Christian solution'
to this universal problem. Death no longer looms as the final
point on the continuum of life. The very cosmos itself has
undergone a transformation and it is no longer subject to the
bondage into which it fell with the fall away from God which
occurred with the entrance of sin into the world (cf. Romans
8:18–25). To be sure, Paul sees this liberation through the
'prism' of the resurrected Christ as the Lord of creation, and
thus allows for a certain 'waiting' and longing for this reality
to be consummated.

So we too, Paul argues, have received the 'down payment'
(Greek *arrabon*) on this redemption through the Holy Spirit,
who is the Spirit of the resurrected Lord himself (cf. Ephesians

1:13, 14). Yet we too 'long' for our redemption, even though it be through death.

Put as simply as possible, the resurrection of Christ did not 'change' death itself into something other than what it is as an end of our mortal existence. There is no basis to expect that Christians should be exempt from the experience of death, nor can the death of Christians ordinarily be expected to be any less traumatic and painful as a physical experience than the death of any human being. To teach otherwise is to mislead people and to remove from them the consolation and strength of Christ precisely when it is most needed. This is not to say that the death of Christians is no different from the death of those who die without knowledge of the benefits of Christ. But the difference is that of a perspective, not that of a physical, or even emotional experience. The degree to which this Christian perspective on dying actually affects the experience of death itself will be considered in chapter 7.

What has been changed through the resurrection of Christ is the trajectory of the human person through the passage-way of death. Viewed apart from Christ's resurrection, death remains the final word and the mortal end to the time and history of each individual. The trajectory of life is relentlessly directed towards the end of life as a personal value in the experience of death. Protests against this fact are evident in every culture with attempts to soften this terror or to imagine an afterlife in which personal identity continues in some form or fashion.

Through the incarnation of God in the form of human flesh, this trajectory was radically altered. This was not apparent in the fact of Jesus' death, as the despair and resignation of the disciples bore witness. It was the resurrection of Jesus which revealed the fact that death had not destroyed the personal time and history of Jesus of Nazareth. His human time and history had come to share in the eternal time and history of God. Jesus of Nazareth, once mortal and finite in his humanity, now lives forever as the life of the eternal Son in fellowship with the Father and the Spirit (cf. Philippians 2:5–1–10).

A Christian perspective on death will be one which both challenges death as a final determination of life and also one which sees death as a servant of God's will. This is expressed poignantly by Dietrich Bonhoeffer in a circular letter to his dispersed Finkenwalde students on the occasion of the death of several former students who were conscripted into the German army. This letter, dated 15 August 1941, included the following reflection on death:

> In the face of death we cannot say in a fatalistic way, 'It is God's will'; we must add the opposite: 'It is not God's will'. Death shows that the world is not what it should be, but that it needs redemption. Christ alone overcomes death. Here, 'It is God's will' and 'It is not God's will' come to the most acute paradox and balance each other out. God agrees to be involved in something that is not his will, and from now on death must serve God despite itself... Only in the cross and resurrection of Jesus Christ has death come under God's power, must it serve the purpose of God. Not a fatalistic surrender, but living faith in Jesus Christ, who died and has risen again for us, can seriously make an end of death for us.[15]

Let me state the fundamental thesis once more. The death and resurrection of Jesus Christ affects our life and death by placing us within the context of that new history of life and death which extends through death to eternal life with God, as experienced in the life of the Son with the Father. It is Jesus of Nazareth who anchors us within that eternal life, by giving us his own Spirit and life.

'If the Spirit of him who raised Jesus from the dead dwells in you, he who raised Christ Jesus from the dead will give life to your mortal bodies also through his Spirit which dwells in you' (Romans 8:11).

The New Testament's answer to the problem of our death is that the victory over death which was achieved in the resurrection of Jesus was a victory for all persons who are related to God through Jesus Christ. The answer is to be found in the reality of the Spirit of the resurrected Christ who comes to those who still face death and bestows the gift of a new creation, a new time and history. To 'die in Christ', as the Apostle now thinks of it, is to have one's entire life upheld by the life of the one who was born, who died, and who continues to live beyond the power of death.

'From now on,' says Paul, 'we regard no one from a human point of view; even though we once regarded Christ from a human point of view, we regard him thus no longer' (2

Corinthians 5:16). By this Paul seems to mean that the old perspective of a human time and history which is orientated towards death, now has given way to a new perspective, a new time and history which is that of the risen and glorified Christ. 'Therefore, if any one is in Christ, he is a new creation; the old has passed away, behold, the new has come' (5:17).

Not only is the risen Christ the Lord of the new community, but, according to Paul, he is Lord of all creation (Ephesians 1:10). It is not that death has been removed as a threat, with the old time and history still left to run its course under the limitations of unredeemed time and space. But time and space, and therefore the time and history of all humanity, has been brought within the continuum of the 'life time' of Jesus Christ.

It is here that sin can be judged in the concreteness and particularity of its consequence for human existence through conformity to Christ's own death and it is here that atonement is made for sin so that sin is no longer 'counted' against those for whom Christ lived and died (2 Corinthians 5:19). The assurance God gave to all people that this event of salvation holds good is that He raised from the dead the one who took the consequences of sin to the absolute and total end – death and estrangement from God. 'But as it is, he has appeared once for all at the end of the age to put away sin by the sacrifice of himself. . . so Christ, having been offered once to bear the sins of many, will appear a second time, not to deal with sin but to save those who are eagerly waiting for him' (Hebrews 9:26, 28).

The fact that Jesus Christ has been raised from the dead is, therefore, not a fact that changes my death as a physical reality. No metaphysical connections can be made with this event which will effect a change in my biological life and death. The connection is through the Spirit of Jesus. It is through the indwelling of the Spirit of this resurrected man that our personal and spiritual existence is transformed 'from death to life' (Romans 8:1–9).

This is the Spirit that he breathed upon his disciples in the upper room on the evening of the first Easter day (John 20:22). It is significant that he approaches them 'on the evening of that day' (20:19), showing us that Easter time continues to allow a structure of temporal time to exist. But even more significant is the fact that it is the Spirit of Jesus of Nazareth, one who had become familiar to them through his own 'life time' which is given to them.

This connection is then given further release into the world through the coming of the Holy Spirit at Pentecost, an event which Jesus himself promised. Thus, Paul can say, 'you are in the Spirit'; 'the Spirit of God dwells in you;' 'you have the 'Spirit of Christ;' 'Christ is in you;' and 'the Spirit of Him who raised Christ Jesus from the dead' will give life to your mortal bodies (Romans 8:9–11). It is through the Spirit of God that we are brought into the continuum of the new time and history of Jesus Christ, and we share in that life which is his by virtue of his having overcome the power of death.

This new time and history is still 'hid with Christ in God' (Colossians 3:3). From outside the perspective of Easter, there is no apparent reality to this life through and beyond death. But for those who have received the Spirit of the resurrected one, there is a view 'beyond death' even as it is a new perspective on our temporal life itself.

There was no Christian burial and no Christian address given on the occasion of Stephen's violent death. He preached his own funeral sermon: 'But he, full of the Holy Spirit, gazed into heaven and saw the glory of God, and Jesus standing at the right hand of God; and he said, "Behold, I see the heavens opened, and the Son of man standing at the right hand of God. . . Lord Jesus, receive my spirit."' (Acts 7:55, 56, 59).

For Stephen, the question we have been asking was answered. Perhaps his answer is ours as well.

NOTES

1 *Systematic Theology* (Chicago: University of Chicago Press, 1957), volume 2, pp. 153ff.

2 *I Believe in the Resurrection of Jesus* (Grand Rapids: Eerdmans, 1975), p. 58. Cf. also, T. F. Torrance, *Space, Time and Resurrection* (Grand Rapids: Eerdmans, 1976), who argues that the resurrection of Jesus radically transformed existing concepts of resurrection. That is to say, the resurrection of Jesus as an event within time and history has no precedent in prevailing concepts of a general resurrection (p. 35). This same criticism can be made of W. Pannenberg's argument that the resurrection of Jesus can be seen as consistent with ideas of resurrection in later Judaism (cf. *Jesus – God and Man* (London: SCM Press, 1968), pp. 74–88.

3 *Space, Time and Resurrection*, p. 164.

4 For a discussion of contingency, especially as understood in its theological implications, see T. F. Torrance, *Divine and Contingent Order* (Oxford: Oxford University Press, 1981).

5 *Space, Time and Resurrection*, p. 175.

6 Ibid., pp. 178–9.

7 *On the Theology of Death* (New York: Herder and Herder, 1967), p. 61.

8 Ibid., pp. 63ff. One cannot help but note that Rahner's view of redemption is similar in some respects to that of Irenaeus, who viewed Adam as an 'incomplete' human being moving toward his perfection as created to be in the image and likeness of God. Gustaf Wingren, commenting on this view of Irenaeus, says, 'Between the child (Adam) and the man (perfected humanity) stands the Son. Jesus, as the Son of God, bearing Adam's flesh brought the humanity of Adam (all men) into a state of health, and removed the 'injury' which occurred through the fall. . . Uncorrupted human life ends in *resurrection* – lordship over death – by the same inner ᵣecessity which brought Adam's perverted life to end in death. . . The conflict which Jesus had to undergo for His life to be fully human and the reverse of Adam's embraced the Resurrection also, and not merely the period up to his death.' *Man and the Incarnation* (Edinburgh/London: Oliver and Boyd, 1959), p. 127.

9 *Foundations of Christian Faith.* (New York: Seabury Press, 1978), pp. 438–9.

10 Ibid., p. 436.

11 *Space, Time and Resurrection*, p. 79.

12 Ibid., pp. 98–9.

13 *Church Dogmatics*, volume 3, part 2, pp. 437ff. The page

references in the text which follows are from this volume. Helmut Thielicke has also recently argued that the resurrection of Christ constitutes a centre within history which gives a new perspective of time. *Being Human. . . Becoming Human* (Garden City, NY: Doubleday, 1984), pp. 315ff.

14 *Death: The Riddle and the Mystery* (Philadelphia: Westminster Press, 1974), pp. 119ff.

15 Cited in *True Patriotism*, (London: Collins, 1973), pp. 124–5.

CHAPTER 6

Christian Hope and Life Beyond Death

We put our sentiments on grave markers and our speculations into theology. REST IN PEACE, urges the inscription on the stone. But before the grass has time to cover the freshly turned earth, the activities of the deceased in the afterlife become a subject of speculation and concern.

During the Middle Ages the subject of death and the afterlife were matters of intense concern in the western world. Fear of death and speculation concerning what would happen afterwards gripped the imagination and inspired literary and theological works. Dante's *Inferno* is but a small fragment of the body of work, comprising plays, books and art works, which graphically depicted the torments of the damned and the pleasures of the good.

The concept of purgatory, as a place where purification of the soul from unremitted sins had to occur, burdened the living with emotional and financial stress. Not only did one have to earn enough to live, but also to pay off the 'spiritual mortgage' for the dead as well!

With the Protestant reformation, much of the superstition and unbiblical speculation regarding the state of the dead in the afterlife was discarded. While this freedom from the medieval mind gave permission for rationalism and the philosophers of the enlightenment to focus more on the nature of life before death, the concept of the immortality of the soul was not immediately abandoned.

The English philosopher David Hume made the first serious attack on belief in the survival of life after death. Stressing the empirical reality of the five senses, Hume regarded concepts of human life as impossible apart from a structure of sensory experience. A decline in the concept of an afterlife reached its climax in the mid-eighteenth century, according to the Church historian Phillip Schaff.[1] A wave of empiricism and scepticism swept through the Continent as well as into the United States.

By the middle of the nineteenth century, people had become bored with the metaphysical exercises of the sceptics, and found the implications of empiricist arguments self-defeating and irrelevant to the texture of real life. There ensued a revived interest in the human personality and the rich experiences of life not capable of being accounted for through scientific and philosophical rationalism.

The mind of the contemporary person, despite the pervasive doctrines of scientific empiricism and secular materialism, continues to be preoccupied with questions about life after death. After reviewing some of these concerns I want to take up three specific theological questions: (1) the issue of personal identity after death; (2) the status of the individual between death and resurrection; and (3) the nature of the resurrection body. The aim of this chapter is to show how the death and resurrection of Jesus Christ provides an answer to some of these contemporary concerns.

One of the first books to turn public interest back towards speculation about the afterlife was *The Coming Race*, by Bulmer-Lytton. His work was of some influence in the thought of such writers as Mathers, Yeats, Crowly and Waite. His book, however, introduced again a view of the afterlife which was more related to the occult practices and superstitions of the Middle Ages than to a biblical view of life after death. His works, says Robert Morey, made the occult fashionable in British society for the first time.[2]

This preoccupation with the occult was associated with the development of a new public consciousness regarding death. The state of those who have died is no longer a matter of speculation and imagination. It is no longer a matter of invading the realm of the dead through dramatic depiction. Through the realm of psychic phenomena the dead themselves will be 'awakened' and encouraged to invade the realm of the living. REST IN PEACE may still be a sentiment expressed on grave stones, but the dead themselves will not be allowed to sleep while others are awake!

The initial spark which ignited public interest in communicating with the dead can be attributed to the séances held by the Fox sisters, who lived in Hydesdale, New York. On 31 March 1848, they conducted a séance in which the spirit of a murdered man was supposedly contacted, who informed them that his corpse could be found in the basement. This proved to be true; a body was found.

The 'spirit' of the dead person was thought to make its presence known through a 'rapping' sound on the table. This led to the fad of 'table rapping' séances which became fashionable, almost as a parlour game.

Some of the most distinguished poets, writers, politicians, philosophers and even scientists, became firm believers in the survival of the human spirit after death through this new movement.

The Society for Psychical Research (SPR) was founded in 1882, and Henry Sedgwich, a noted philosopher at Cambridge, was instrumental in gathering influential people into this society. The membership included such men as William Gladstone (former prime minister), Arthur Balfour (future prime minister), Alfred Lord Tennyson, Lewis Carroll, Sir Arthur Conan Doyle (the creator of Sherlock Holmes), and C. D. Broad (philosopher).[3]

The SPR investigated occult experiences in a scientific manner, seeking to expose fraudulent ones and to establish claims which must be seen as valid. In investigating over 17,000 cases, they dismissed all but 1,684. By this means, they sought to provide evidence that humans did indeed survive death, and existed as conscious persons who could communicate with persons still alive.

This fad died out in the early part of the twentieth century. New forms of scepticism and empiricism pressed towards what has been called 'secular humanism', with an emphasis on materialism and with a disdain for questions which had to do with 'spirits' and the afterlife.

One important outcome of this movement, however, is represented in the work of Joseph Banks Rhine. Born in 1895, he was trained as a biologist at the University of Chicago, drinking deep at the well of the emerging scepticism and empiricism in that environment. He heard a lecture by Sir Arthur Conan Doyle, however, who planted in his mind the idea of discovering a scientific proof for a conscious afterlife. Becoming involved with the SPR while a faculty member at

Harvard University, Rhine, along with William McDougall, later developed a department of psychic studies at Duke University.

Because the concepts involved with the séance, with its manifestation and terminology of the occult, were unacceptable to Rhine, he set out to re-define or re-label the subjects which SPR had researched for years. It was Rhine who coined the term ESP – extrasensory perception. Other terms, such as 'para-normal psychology', or 'parapsychology' were developed out of this new research. Despite setbacks and misleading attempts to prove that a horse was 'telepathic', Rhine's work led to serious research and study of the phenomenon of human consciousness as existing 'outside' of or beyond the limits of the material body. The Russians conducted psychic research experiments of their own, and their findings were released in a popularized form in *Psychic Discoveries Behind the Iron Curtain* by Sheila Ostrander and Lynn Schroeder (Prentice-Hall, 1970).[4]

We seem to have come full circle, with one notable difference. The medieval concern for life after death was a belief in the supernatural which relied upon religious belief and the reality of God as the basis for this belief. The contemporary preoccupation with evidences for conscious life outside of the body and even beyond death, is not dependent upon religious belief and, if these concepts can be said to be belief in the supernatural, they can also be found, in many cases, to be held by atheists. Belief in God is not now necessary to support belief in life after death as a personal and conscious existence of the same person.

From the eastern cultures, the theory of reincarnation, of course, has been the predominate mode of conceptualizing life after death. 'The idea that we have lived many times before and must live many times again,' says John Hick, 'seems as self-evident to most people in the Hindu and Buddhist east as the contrary idea that we came into existence at conception or birth, and shall see the last of this world at death.'[5] The assumption of the Judaeo-Christian view that souls are not eternal and that a new soul comes into existence whenever a new person is born seems utterly implausible and unreasonable to the eastern mind, Professor Hick goes on to say.

The various theories of reincarnation as held, for example,

by the more popular mind, as compared with those held in Vedantic and Buddhist philosophies, are too complex to discuss here.[6] What is held in common, is that the soul, as the conscious character- and memory-bearing self, can assume one or more bodies in succession. Thus, death is a 'transmigration of the soul', one might say, from a body which is perishing to another body which can sustain the life of the self. The degree to which personal identity can be said to be sustained, however, is dependent upon the form of the reincarnation theory.

For the connecting thread of memory to be lost, Hick argues, would seriously weaken the assumption that personal identity is maintained through the series of reincarnations. The belief that these memories are actually suppressed, and can be brought to consciousness through hypnosis, is the theory most widely known as reincarnation in the popular form. We shall have more to say about the problem of personal identity and reincarnation later in the chapter when we look more carefully at Hick's own view with regard to life after death.

One further development needs to be reported before we examine the issues these concepts raise from a theological perspective. The recent work of the Swiss-born American psychiatrist, Elizabeth Kübler-Ross, and her pioneering book *On Death and Dying* (1969) stimulated a great deal of interest in life after death possibilities. This interest was heightened with the publication of *Questions and Answers on Death and Dying* (1974), and the recounting of testimonies of persons who had death or 'near-death' experiences in which the person was conscious of being outside of the body while supposedly clinically dead. These experiences included reports of visiting places which left impressions of great peacefulness, of seeing a tunnel of light, and even of what was described as 'heaven' and 'hell'.

The first serious studies of near-death experiences, however, were conducted by a prominent Swiss geologist, Albert Heim. After a near-fatal fall in the Alps, during which he had a mystical experience, he became interested in situations reported by others. Over a period of decades, he collected observations and reports from numerous survivors of serious accidents. He first reported his findings to a meeting of the Swiss Alpine Club in 1892. In his report, he said that in most cases where death or life-threatening situations were experienced, mental activity was enhanced, time became greatly expanded, the individual experienced a 'life review,' and there were often experiences of transcendental beauty and the sound of 'celestial' music.[7]

In 1961, Karlis Osis and his co-workers analysed more than 600 questionnaires returned by physicians and nurses who detailed the experiences of their patients in clinical 'near-death' situations. The typical experience was one of tranquillity, with vivid images of indescribable beauty, often including religious concepts, such as paradise or heaven. Osis pointed out the similarity of these terminal experiences to effects caused by psychedelic drugs. This has led, of course, to research and use of such drugs as a means of easing the distress of dying in patients. In fact, as the Grofs have pointed out, comparative studies of the concepts of the afterlife have revealed far-reaching similarities among different ethnic and religious groups. Modern consciousness-research has shown that these similarities can be reproduced by drugs in psychedelic sessions. These experiences, thus, tend to belong to the continuum of psychic experience, which have proved, not life after death, but that the relation between the conscious self and the embodied self is more complex than previously thought.[8]

This brief review of contemporary approaches to the question of life after death suggests that there are issues which are of vital concern to people on a broad spectrum of life. The subject is not one which is unique to Christian theology, nor are these issues restricted to those who hold religious assumptions concerning the matter of death and the hereafter.

The concern of this chapter, however, is to reflect upon these issues from the perspective of Christian theology. Our particular concern is to trace out the implications of the death and resurrection of Jesus Christ as a way of developing a theology of life after death.

Three issues seem to be of concern to the contemporary mind, even as they were also issues which rose, to some degree, in the minds of the early Christians. These are (1) the issues of personal identity in life after death; (2) the status of the human person between death and resurrection; and (3) what the nature of life in a resurrected body might be.

What is the issue with regard to identity? What is at stake is the meaning of survival of the individual person through the death of the physical body. If indeed there is a resurrection, this will be of a 'different kind' of body, according to the Apostle Paul (1 Corinthians 15:35–44). If we conceive of a person as essentially an immortal soul, along with the Greeks, then there is no basic problem. The soul is the centre of personal identity, and it continues uninterrupted through death into its new form of disembodied life. If, however, we hold that the identity of a person is somehow connected with the body, then how can we be the same person, with a quite different body? The concept of resurrection entails some kind of discontinuity, or gap in the personal identity of an individual.

The argument for continued personal identity in life after death as a logical premise has been made most consistently, though not always convincingly, in recent times by John Hick. In response to the challenge of Anthony Flew, that religious claims are cognitively meaningless unless they are capable of falsification, Hick argued that the Christian concept of an afterlife is capable of verification on logical grounds alone, even though not falsifiable.[9]

The hypothesis of the resurrection of the body and of continued personal identity of the same subject through the discontinuity of death, according to Hick, is verifiable though it is not falsifiable. It is verifiable in the sense that the concept of continued personal identity under these circumstances does not violate logical consistency of thought. As a consequence, he argues, the Pauline concept of personal immortality through resurrection is highly reasonable as a concept of 'eschatological verification'. Hick feels that he has demonstrated that the concept of a resurrection body is not logically inconsistent with a definition of personal existence. The final verification, of course, will come through the actual experience of resurrection following death. Thus, it is 'eschatological verification'.

In discussing Hick's argument, Douglas Walton has raised questions about a serious ambivalence in Hick's theory. For Hick, says Walton, the question of identity in terms of a resurrection body which is quite unlike a mortal body are central. However, Walton says, for the sceptic, the concern is not so much for logical consistency in such a thesis, but that an 'enormous evasion' has taken place. The epistemology of death as an empirical experience, suggests Walton, defies resolution because there is no verifiable *experience* of death, much less verifiable experience of life after death of an embodied sort. Thus, the Pauline doctrine of the resurrection of the body as constituting the basis for continued personal identity beyond death slips out of Hick's grasp in his attempt to verify a *concept* of immortality as a logically consistent hypothesis.[10]

In his later work, Hick returns to the theme of personal identity as central to the concept of life after death. There are three strands of continuity necessary for personal identity, he suggests – memory, bodily continuity and psychological continuity.[11] If the connecting thread of personal memory is broken through death, as well as bodily continuity, this only leaves psychological continuity in the form of a pattern of mental dispositions. In a theory of reincarnation which holds that there is an 'unconscious memory' bank, Hick suggests, then two of the three strands can be sustained, and personal identity may be affirmed as possible.

The fact is, Hick suggests, the question of personal identity depends upon how one asks the question and for what purpose. When the question is put in terms of the relation of personal identity to physical identity, the question has clear and unproblematic boundaries. With no continued physical existence there can be no continued personal identity after death. If, however, one asks the question from the standpoint of subjective identity apart from physical identity, the question of identity has variable and misty horizons.[12]

Drawing upon concepts from an eastern religious anthropology, Hick proposes that we view the matter of personal identity in terms of a three-fold interaction between body, mind (soul) and spirit, or 'Atman'. The concept of 'Atman' is that of the supra-individual constituent of personhood. The embodied mind (soul) consists of a self enclosed individual possessing 'egoity', seeking its own identity over and against other 'egos'. The 'Atman', however, as the spirit of personal identity, is the unconscious unity of the self with the community of personal being which constitutes our true personal identity.[13]

As a third alternative to either traditional concepts of bodily resurrection or reincarnation, Hick proposes a continuation of life after death in the form of a 'series of lives, each bounded by something analogous to birth and death, lived in other worlds in spaces other than that in which we now are'.[14] In this way, he hopes to provide a 'global theology of death' which will provide a synthesis between the traditional doctrine of resurrection to an individual personal life and the eastern concepts of reincarnation.

The process of overcoming 'egoity' as a means of experiencing personal identity, says Hick, may require many stages of development following this 'first life' in our present embodied form. Is it fair to say, then, that Hick has accepted the theory of reincarnation? Probably not. Although we must immediately add that he has only modified the traditional concepts of reincarnation. Hick has in view a continued series of 'births and deaths' following physical death, leading to the goal of a personal existence in the form of the 'Atman'. This appears to be quite similar to the eastern concept of undifferentiated consciousness.

On the other hand, it would not be fair to Hick to say that he has abandoned differentiation as an essential aspect of personal being beyond death. While the concept of Atman replaces that of egoity for him, it is not entirely clear just what degree of differentiation Atman will yield when there is a final union of consciousness in community.

> I have used the name atman for this deeper or higher consciousness or self, of which human individuals are constituent aspects – separated now by egoity but finally to be united in a perfect community of personal relationships – because the idea of the ultimate oneness of mankind, although not confined to the religions of Indian origin has been most explicitly affirmed by them.[15]

Perhaps we might conclude that the form of differentiation by which personal identity is maintained beyond death in Hick's view is more of a logical distinction than a material one. In which case, the problem of identity now suffers a new dilemma. For if there is no clear continuity between identity as a material possession and experience of the self and a formal distinction or differentiation, one is still not assured that the Atman is a replica of the ego, to use Hick's own concepts.

For all of the quite obvious elements of an eastern philosophy of being in Hick's proposal, which views individuality as a lesser form of being than a unity of being in which individuality as egoity is dissolved, one can find much of the same in Paul Tillich.

Asserting that God is not a person, but the personal, and that God is not a being, but the ground of all being, Tillich tells us that our finitude does not cease to be finitude, but is 'taken into' the infinite, the eternal being of God. Tillich argues that the Christian emphasis on the individual person will not permit an 'absorption' into the One infinite being. Yet it is not altogether clear what this means when he denies both the concept of resurrection of the body and of the immortality of the soul. The problem with the concept of resurrection, Tillich proposes, is that it suggests the survival of the person as a self conscious individual.

What seems to be an ambivalence within Tillich's own thought may be seen as the problem of the relation of the eternal to time in his fundamental concept of reality. 'The Eternal is not a future state of things. It is always present, not only in man (who is aware of it), but also in everything that has being within the whole of being'. Yet, he can also say, 'Eternal life is still life and the universal centredness does not dissolve the individual centres.'[16] So too, along with Hick, Tillich does not wish to dissolve personal differentiation completely. Yet, the end result is the same. Where Hick has a logical distinction between the self as Atman and as a centre of egoity, Tillich offers an existential distinction between the self as temporal and the self as eternal. The issue of continuity of personal identity in both cases remains in doubt.

If Tillich indeed is denying the survival of the person as a self conscious individual, as he appears to do, this may justify the comment of H.D. Lewis that 'the proper place for Tillich and many of his followers today is in the Hindu religion'.[17]

We cannot avoid a glance at the curious suggestion of Karl Rahner that the survival of the soul after death takes place in the form of a 'pancosmic' event. As such, the soul does not escape the cosmos, but the cosmos becomes the new 'body' of the soul. The metaphysics of this view are no less obscure in many ways than those of Tillich, but Rahner makes quite clear that he is not thinking of a continued survival of individual self conscious identity apart from this world, but of an openness of the being of the self to the entire cosmic reality.

In this pancosmic existence, the person after death experiences resurrection as the 'glorified body' of the cosmos as a whole. In this way, Rahner says, we may understand the concept of purgatory as a process by which the soul is freed progressively from the disharmony which it experienced while in the temporal body in order to achieve maturity and total openness to its harmony with the entire cosmos. The doctrine of the resurrection in this view, is understood as a 'pancosmic corporeality'. 'A corporeality which is the actual expression of spirit, though concrete, remains open for maintaining or entering into free and unhampered relations with everything' says Rahner.[18]

Rahner does not appear to go so far as either Hick or Tillich in altering the concept of a future existence as a differentiated personal being.[19] But one is quite at a loss to give actual content to the concept of 'pancosmic' personal existence, where each person touches the whole and where the whole comprises the 'embodied' form of each person. Does this metaphysical concept of personal existence viewed through the prism of a cosmic whole really contain the substance of what the Apostle Paul said to the Corinthians as a response to their questions about the nature of the resurrection experience (1 Corinthians 15)? This remains to be seen.

What is quite obvious by its omission in the attempts that we have considered to define personal identity in the afterlife, is the biblical reference to the personal identity of Jesus of Nazareth in his own resurrection body. It is of significant concern to the authors of the four gospels that the readers understand that the disciples needed to be convinced that it was indeed the same Jesus whom they had known as the one crucified that they encountered in his resurrection body. Luke takes special pains to impress upon us the fact that the disciples needed to be convinced that it was truly Jesus himself whom they experienced, and not some glorious apparition from another sphere. Jesus said to the disciplines, 'Why are you troubled, and why do questionings arise in your hearts? See my hands and my feet, that it is I myself; handle me, and see' (Luke 24:38–39). Then he said to them, 'These are my words which I spoke to you, while I was still with you' (24:44).

Here we are not presented with an answer to the question as to why, in principle, an exact identity could be assumed between the pre-crucified and the post-resurrected Jesus. Christian theology holds that there must be *some* form of personal identity between the Jesus who died and the Jesus who confronted the early witnesses after his resurrection. It does not appear to be necessary to Christian faith that this identity be reducible to a physical replica, even with some necessary alterations made. In this we can agree with John Hick that the physical replication of Jesus following the resurrection is not the main point of continuity. Consequently, the biblical testimony to the identity of Jesus following his resurrection must be taken as based on a *sufficient* continuity of personal identity, though not necessarily an exact one in the sense of replication. If they were convinced that it was the *same* Jesus, then they were able to hold as a confession of their own Christian hope that there would be the *same kind* of identity for each of them in the resurrection.

So it is a tenet of Christian theology that the resurrection of Jesus of Nazareth determines the fact that personal identity is continued through death and resurrection. The Apostle encourages the Christians in Philippi to remain hopeful and faithful to the end because, 'our commonwealth is in heaven, and from it we await a Saviour, the Lord Jesus Christ, who will change our lowly body to be like his glorious body, by the power which enables him even to subject all things to himself' (Philippians 3:20–21).

The answer to the question of the survival of personal identity through death is a question that has been answered in the death and resurrection of Jesus Christ, and can only be a question we can ask in this Christological framework. Our personal identity, as Thielicke helpfully reminds us, is not a predication we can make based on our creaturely nature, but is predicated upon the initiative of God who addresses us and upholds us as the persons we are, before him and with each other. 'The constancy of our identity is the constancy of God's faithfulness'.[20]

Though the continuity of our time and history is broken with death, as Paul indicates (1 Corinthians 15:42ff), our personal identity exists because it is grounded in our time and history with God. Thielicke again: 'To all eternity we are those who are called by name. "Those with whom God has begun to speak, whether in wrath or in grace, are immortal" (Luther). . . this means that, since the history with God that is the basis of our identity does not cease, we are upheld in our identity even beyond death.'[21]

The answer to the question: 'Will I exist as the person that I now am, and as I am known by others, in the resurrection from the dead?', comes when we answer the question: 'Do we believe, along with his disciples, that it is the same Jesus of Nazareth whom they knew before his death as appeared to them in his resurrection body?'

So it seems we should not put REST IN PEACE on those grave markers, but UNTIL WE MEET AGAIN.

This, of course, leads us to our second theological question. What does 'until' mean for the one who had died but has not yet been raised from the dead? What is the status of the person who has died between death and resurrection? Is this a conscious, disembodied existence? Or does the soul 'sleep', held suspended in a state of unconscious existence until 'awakened' by resurrection?

Here too, there have been speculations and theories with little unanimity of thought on the matter. Nor are the biblical statements which seem to speak to this issue free from ambiguities. When writing to the church at Thessalonica, Paul assures them that 'God will bring with him those who have fallen asleep' (1 Thessalonians 4:14). The metaphor of sleep is an easy one for Paul to use (cf. I Corinthians 15:6, 18), but not so easy for us to interpret.

To the Corinthians, Paul wrote urging them not to lose heart even though death might overtake them. While we are 'at home in the body we are away from the Lord', but 'we would rather be away from the body and at home with the Lord' (2 Corinthians 5:6, 8). Yet, as he envisions this transition, he appears to shrink from the idea that being 'without the body' he would be 'found naked', and that our desire is not that we should be 'unclothed' (i.e. disembodied), but that we would be 'further clothed' (5:3, 4). Certainly there is no encouragement for Paul in the prospect of an intermediate state between death and resurrection where he would be conscious of being 'unclothed', that is, in a disembodied, conscious state.

With regard to his own situation, he writes to the church at Philippi and says that his great desire is 'to depart and be with Christ, for that is better'. Though he also is willing to 'remain in the flesh' if that means that he can have fruitful service for Christ (Philippians 1:22–24).

Our conclusion is that Paul did not think the question of the status of the person *between* death and resurrection was a question that needed to be considered. For Christians, their death is softened because they 'die in Christ', and thus one should view them as 'sleeping'. The thought seems to be that sleep is a form of continuity of life, not the end of it. There is probably no thought in this use of the metaphor by Paul of the time element involved in sleeping. He can think of dying as 'falling asleep' but also as 'being at home with the Lord' (2 Corinthians 5:8).

Throughout Church history there have been theologians who have held that the soul of the person does indeed sleep in an unconscious existence during the interval between death and resurrection. Luther himself is said to have explored this concept as an alternative to the medieval doctrine of purgatory, but in his later writings clearly repudiated this concept. 'In the interim [between death and resurrection], the soul does not sleep but is awake and enjoys the vision of angels and of God, and has converse with them.'[22] For the most part, it is fair to say that this represents the traditional orthodox view of Protestant theology, with critical exceptions, of course.

There are some denominations, such as the Seventh Day Adventists and groups like the Jehovah's Witnesses, who do hold the doctrine of 'soul sleep'. Some who hold to soul sleep during the intermediate state, also hold to the annihilation of the wicked during this period, with the righteous being raised and given a resurrection body. Others, hold that both the saved and the lost sleep during this period, and both are raised for either eternal life in heaven or eternal torment in hell.

In his discussion of the concept of the intermediate state, which I find most helpful, Thielicke points to the fact that the New Testament is not concerned for a 'state' which exists between death and resurrection, but for a 'relation' which exists between the person and Christ through death. This, of course, is why, as pointed out earlier, there is no speculation on this issue in the New Testament. The problem that arises in the way the question is put has to do with the problem of time and temporality. The dead who are viewed as 'sleeping', says Thielicke, are 'called out of time' in the same sense that one can awaken from sleep with no awareness of time having really passed. Therefore, he argues, 'The removal of a sense of time means for those who are awakened that the long night of death is reduced to a mathematical point, and they are thus summoned out of completed life.'[23]

In this way, the state of those who have died is not described in terms of those who continue to live in the flow of temporality, but in terms of the relationship of that person to Christ. This relation is one of immediacy, with no time interval projected into it at all.

In a similar way, T. F. Torrance says, 'Looked at from the perspective of the new creation there is no gap between the death of the believer and the *parousia* of Christ, but looked at from the perspective of time that decays and crumbles away, there is a lapse of time between them.'[24] Thus we cannot 'think' these two spheres of reality together. We cannot 'synchronize the clock' of eternal time with our temporal time. It is the attempt to do this, in my judgement, which has led to the speculation and unfortunate controversies over the so-called intermediate state.

Our response, then, is to put this issue of the state of those who have died within the Christological framework, and to believe along with Paul, that we will not be found 'naked' or 'unclothed', but that we will be 'further clothed' so that our personal identity will be sustained as embodied self with the same continuity with which Christ himself moved through his death and resurrection. The 'three days', after all, during which he was said to be dead and buried, were the result of a perspective from the time and history of death itself. The 'three days' were a perspective from the history of death. Jesus certainly did not have to spend three days in a disembodied state awaiting a resurrection body. Having been raised by God in the power of the immediate relation which suffered no discontinuity through death, Jesus met them after *their* three days were over.

Hidden in the UNTIL WE MEET AGAIN, therefore, is the eternal NOW. This is true because it is the truth of Christ – the I AM.

We now turn to our third theological question. What will it really be like to have a resurrection body? 'Will there be snow in heaven for us to play in?' my first born daughter asked when we moved out of the frozen landscape of middle America to the perpetual summertime of southern California. 'Of course there will be,' was my answer. 'Streets of gold in the city for those who need that assurance, and snow covered slopes in the countryside for those who anticipate that pleasure!' If heaven is really inconceivable because it is a reality which extends beyond our conception, why not allow imagination to touch the borders, at least, of that which touches our lives at the very centre.

There have indeed been some interesting speculations as to the nature of the resurrection body. Augustine, we are told, though he accepted the Platonic theory of the immortality of the soul, speculated none the less on the precise nature of the resurrection body. It was important to him that the resurrection be both bodily and perfect. In this, of course, he moved in a direction that Plato would have considered totally irrelevant, if not downright silly. The righteous will be restored, Augustine believed, to their most comely appearance. Fetuses will be mature, monsters made normal, unsightly blemishes and deformities corrected, and each person having some recognizable likeness to their former self. However, the thin will not be raised thin, nor the obese in their former obesity.[25] I am afraid it sounds like wishful thinking to me!

Walter Rauschenbusch, the proponent of the social gospel, was strongly moved by the apocalyptic vision which suggested that in the age to come deprivation in this life would be compensated for. This led him to say that in the afterlife, persons with limited education would be able to pursue college level courses![26] Now we have a new question, 'Will there be final examinations in heaven?'

Paul, as we might expect, even though he thought such questions a little foolish, gave a serious and straightforward answer. Using the analogy of the planting of seeds, first of all, he suggests that the kind of transformation which occurs when a kernal of grain decomposes in the soil with the resulting new growth above the ground, points to a similar transformation in the human body through death (1 Corinthians 15:35–38). From this he develops the thesis that 'each seed has its own body'. Presumably, the body which the seed produces, though quite different from the form of the seed itself, is the 'seed's own body'.

Paul then moves to another analogy. Celestial bodies are quite different from terrestial bodies, each with their own 'glory'. So too, he argues, with the resurrection of the dead, the body which is 'sown' is perishable and thus, one could say, inglorious. The body which is raised, on the other hand, while coming from the same 'seed', is now imperishable and glorious (15:40–43).

This clearly points to a radical discontinuity in the nature of the resurrection body from that of the body which is subject to death. Yet, in this discontinuity, there is the continuity of 'kind' for, based on the analogy of the seed, the resurrection body 'belongs' to the person in the same way that the earthly, perishable body belonged to the person.

Paul clearly wishes his readers to be comforted by the fact that their resurrection bodies will be 'their own body' and not merely a new or strange body. But he does not answer the question as to precisely what this resurrection body will look like or how the embodied existence of the resurrection can be understood in terms of our present embodied state.

He does warn us that it would be unthinkable to project concepts based upon our present time and space embodiment into the resurrection: 'I tell you this, brethren: flesh and blood cannot inherit the kingdom of God, nor does the perishable inherit the imperishable' (1 Corinthians 15:50).

I began by saying that we tend to put our sentiments on our grave markers and our speculations into our theology. I have certainly done my share of speculating in this theological discussion, but in the end, it is what we say that we believe that is the better part of our theology.

I want my grave marker to reflect more of what I believe about life after death and my continued existence in the presence of God than my speculations about it. Is there such a thing as a 'tombstone theology?' Maybe so.

'He is not here; for he has risen,' the angel spoke at the tombstone of Jesus. 'Why do you seek the living among the dead?' (Matthew 28:6; Luke 24:5).

'I have fought the good fight,' the apostle wrote as his own epitaph; 'I have finished the race, I have kept the faith. Henceforth there is laid up for me the crown of righteousness, which the Lord, the righteous judge, will award to me on that Day, and not only to me but also to all who have loved his appearing' (2 Timothy 4:7–8).

A good theology of death and the afterlife is one that you can put on your tombstone, not merely in a textbook.

NOTES

1 *History of the Christian Church*, volume 2, pp. 859ff. Cited by Robert A. Morey, *Death and the Afterlife*, (Minneapolis: Bethany House, 1984)p. 174. Morey's discussion of these concepts has been helpful to me in preparing my own comments.
2 Morey, *Death and the Afterlife*, p. 175.
3 Ibid., pp. 175–6.
4 Cf. L. Froom, *The Conditionalist Faith of our Fathers* (Washington, DC: Review and Harald, 1966), volume 1, pp. 917ff; volume 2, p. 63. Cited by Morey, *Death and the Afterlife*, pp. 177ff. For a discussion of ESP as evidence for the existence of the conscious self apart from the body, see John Hick, *Death and Eternal Life* (San Francisco: Harper and Row, 1976), pp. 121ff.
5 *Death and Eternal Life*, p. 297.
6 See Hick's discussion, ibid, pp. 302ff.
7 Cited by Stanislav and Christina Grof, *Beyond Death – the Gates of Consciousness* (New York: Thames and Hudson, 1980), p. 8.
8 Ibid. For further literature on this subject, see *Life After Death*, by Raymond Moody (New York: Bantam Books, 1977), and *Reflections on Life After Death*, by Raymond Moody (New York: Bantam Books, 1978); *Beyond Death's Door*, by Maurice Rawlings (New York: Thomas Nelson, 1981). John J. Heaney, a Roman Catholic theologian, has contributed an important book seeking to create a positive dialogue between theology and parapsychology: *The Sacred and the Psychic: Parapsychology and Christian Theology* (New York: Paulist Press, 1984).
9 Anthony Flew, 'Theology and Falsification', in *New Essays in Philosophical Theology* (London: SCM Press, 1955), pp. 96–9. John Hick, *Faith and Knowledge* (Ithaca, NY: Cornell University Press, 1957; 'Mr. Clarke's Resurrection Also', in *Sophia*, 1972, XI: 1–3.
10 Douglas B. Walton, *On Defining Death* (Montreal: McGill-Queens University Press, 1979), pp. 78–88.
11 *Death and Eternal Life*, pp. 306–7.
12 Ibid., p. 411. The question of the continuity of physical identity through death and resurrection, however, is not as easily handled as Hick seems to indicate. See the essay by Professor Stephen Davis, 'Is Personal Identity Retained in the Resurrection?', in *Modern Theology*, 1986. Davis argues that the identity of human persons as embodied selves may be 'gap inclusive' with regard to the relation of the mortal body to the resurrection body, with no necessary loss of embodied personal identity. Patrick Sherry has recently contributed to this discussion by reflecting upon the role

which the 'Saints' play in the religious tradition of immortality: *Spirit, Saints, and Immortality* (Albany, NY: State University of New York Press, 1984). See especially pp. 78ff.

13 *Death and Eternal Life*, pp. 450, 462.

14 Ibid, p. 456.

15 Ibid, p. 462.

16 *Systematic Theology* (Chicago: Chicago University Press, 1963), Volume 3, pp. 411, 400, 401.

17 *World Religions*, H. D. Lewis and R. L. Slater (London: Watts, 1966), p. 195. Cited by R. Aldwinckle, *Death in the Secular City* (Grand Rapids: Eerdmans, 1972), p. 90.

18 *On the Theology of Death* (New York: Herder and Herder, 1967), pp. 25–6. For Rahner's discussion of pancosmic identity, see pp. 21ff.

19 For John Hick's discussion and criticism of Rahner's view of the afterlife, see *Death and Eternal Life*, pp. 228ff.

20 H. Thielicke, *Being Human . . . Becoming Human* (Garden City, NY: Doubleday, 1984), p. 89.

21 Thielicke, ibid., p. 91. See also Thielicke's comments on the survival of personal identity in *Living With Death* (Grand Rapids: Eerdmans, 1983), pp. 116ff.

22 Luther, *Commentary on Genesis*, p. 223. Cited by R. Morey, *Death and the Afterlife*, p. 201. For an extended discussion of the concept of the intermediate state, see pp. 199ff in Morey.

23 *Living With Death*, pp. 176–7.

24 T. F. Torrance, *Space, Time and Resurrection* (Grand Rapids: Eerdmans, 1976), p. 102.

25 *Enchiridion*, xxiii, 89ff., *Library of Christian Classics*, volume VII. Cited by James Carse, *Death and Existence* (New York: John Wiley, 1980), p. 251.

26 In *A Theology for the Social Gospel* (New York: Abingdon Press, 1917); 'The social gospel would add the kindred fact that a further large proportion of individuals are left so underdeveloped by our earthly social security system that they deserve a heavenly post-graduate course to make it up for them. It would be a great joy in heaven to find men trooping in from mines and shops, and women from restuarant kitchens and steaming laundries, and getting their long delayed college education' (p. 237).

CHAPTER 7

Christian Perspectives on Death and Dying

'Every idea about death is a version of life.'[1] There are no different degrees or kinds of death, only the circumstances are exceptional. The death of a child only differs from the death of an aged person with respect to the criteria of life. The way in which a person dies is a fact of life, not of death. The violent death of a victim of murder, the slow death produced by malnutrition, the quiet death which occurs during sleep – these all have in common the same final end, death.

It is in our versions of life that we find the true variables. If there is such a thing as a Christian perspective on death, as contrasted with other perspectives, this is a perspective on life. There is no such thing as a Christian death, or a Jewish death, or even an atheist death. There is only death, which by definition is always the same – the end of life.

Jesus had very little to say about death. The Sermon on the Mount contains instructions for living, but not one instruction concerning death. Jesus expressed outrage over the religious pretensions of the Pharisees, but none over the death of innocent children. Are we to think that there were no atrocities, no death of children through starvation or neglect, no victims of senseless accidents or violent crimes? Hardly.

How do we explain his silence when John the Baptist lost his head over the whim of Herod? What do we make of his response when told of the Galileans who lost their lives and whose blood was mingled with that of their sacrifices by Pilate? (Luke 13:1–5) Why no cry for justice, why no outrage against their untimely and unfortunate death?

We can only conclude that Jesus accepted death as a matter of fact which did not require an interpretation of its own. His concern was for life and for what one did with one's life with respect to the Kingdom of God. Yet, we know that he wept when confronted with the death of his friend Lazarus (John 11:35), and expressed compassion for the grieving of the widow whose only son had died (Luke 7:13). When confronted with death itself, he intervened and raised the dead. But this was meant to be a manifestation of his messianic power as one sent from God, not a polemic against death itself.

Of his own death, he only expressed a steadfastness of conviction that he must continue the direction his life had taken as the obedient Son of the Father, even if that meant death. Even here, he had no teaching concerning death, especially that of his own, but his teaching was that of life. 'Whoever would save his life will lose it; and whoever loses his life for my sake, he will save it. . . I must go on my way today and tomorrow and the day following; for it cannot be that a prophet should perish away from Jerusalem' (Luke 9:24; 13:33).

Following the death and resurrection of Christ, as we have seen, the early Christian community understood that the time and history of life had now been extended through death. As a result, the power of death to destroy life has been overcome through Christ. Christians still die in the same manner as they did before Christ died and was raised; and the death of Christians occurred in a manner not unlike the death of other persons. There were unfortunate, tragic, violent and untimely deaths, and one must assume the death of children, within the early Christian community.

Death itself, however, has been relativized to the new order of time and history following Easter. The discontinuity of death was viewed as overcome through the continuity of a relationship with the living Christ, whom they understood to be the 'first born of the dead'. He is now the one who can say, 'I died, and behold I am alive for evermore, and I have the keys of Death and Hades' (Revelation 1:5, 18). The crown of life is promised to those who are now 'faithful unto death' (2:10).

The history of the Christian church and its view of death has been the continued exegesis of the risen Christ as the basic text for life. Thus Karl Barth can say that death itself is to be accepted as part of the free action by which God gives each person life.

It is His gift. It is grace which He shows to man but does not owe
to man; grace by which He binds us but not Himself. This is
revealed in human death. He is still the God from whom man is,
even when He lets man die. Thus in death and above death, He
is still the hope of man. He is the one hope of man, not only in
His death – for death only discloses the fact – but in his life.[2]

The core of this Christian perspective on life and death is faith.
It is faith in the God who has overcome death and who lives
through Jesus Christ that enables Christians to surrender
their time and history to God and to receive it back again from
Him as the gift of life through death.

When we look, for example, at the way in which contemporary Judaism views death, we can see a distinctive difference.
For the Jew, continuity of history itself through the projection
of the race constitutes the only 'redemption' from death. Death
is the end of the individual person, but the corporate personality of the Jew continues. Death is thus an inevitability for the
Jew which does not and must not break the continuity of
history itself.

This is why the holocaust is such a theological problem for
the Jew. If the holocaust is not merely an accident of history,
but an expression of it, then the history of the Jewish people as
a sign of God's promise of life is called into question. 'If the
Exodus led to Sinai, then where does Auschwitz lead?', asks
Jacob Neusner.[3] Some contemporary Jews, like Richard
Rubinstein, conclude that Auschwitz leads to the death of God.
Thus, the inevitability of death is also coupled with the
inevitability of the loss of Jewish identity.

Other Jews, however, protest against this interpretation of
the holocaust as an inevitability of history, and thus of the
death of God. Emil Fackenheim argues that Hitler must not be
given a 'posthumous victory' by allowing the history of the Jew
to perish. 'A Jew may not respond to Hitler's attempt to destroy
Judaism by himself cooperating in its destruction.'[4]

The modern Jew, therefore, will have a version of death
which is derived out of a perspective on life. If life is a
continuation of history with God through continued dialogue
with God, then death cannot destroy this life, even though the
individual perishes. Death cannot destroy the Jew, in this
view, as long as there are Jews to die.

This is in sharp contrast to the Christian version of death which is derived out of a perspective of life as resting in the continuity of God, not in temporal history. Christians do not view immortality as the projection of history, but as the gift of God who is in a contingent, not a necessary relation to history. If God becomes identified with history rather than with the persons who make history, then the death of God is inevitable along with the death of the individual in history.

The discontinuity of death, for Christians, is indeed the discontinuity of temporal history. However, through the incarnation of God within history in the *person* of Jesus Christ, personal identity is broken free from the inevitability of history as a history of death. The resurrection of Jesus Christ enables the Christian to maintain a perspective of continuity of personal life through this new time and history. This is the significance of the Christian doctrine of the Holy Spirit as the personal indwelling of Christ himself within individuals as well as a reality of Christian community. For the Christian community as the existence of the Church within history cannot provide the continuity needed to sustain the future identity of the person.

If the Church as a historical institution is seen as the continuity of the individual, then the inevitability of the death of the Church and the failure of the Christian religion to answer the ultimate questions of life will mean the loss of personal identity. It can even mean the death of God. This will then put the Christian perspective in the same plane as the modern Jewish perspective when continuity with history is not related to the resurrection history of the risen and exalted Christ. It is, therefore, no accident of history which placed Richard Rubinstein in the same company as Thomas Altizer and William Hamilton in the contemporary 'Death of God' movement.

This book takes the position that there is a Christian perspective of life which is developed out of the death and resurrection of Jesus Christ. What has been set forth thus far is an attempt to present this foundation. From this perspective, theological reflection can take place on the issues which death raises for us.

Of necessity we must limit our discussion to selected issues. In discussing these issues, we are not attempting to survey the literature regarding them, nor are we suggesting that the last word is being said concerning them from a Christian perspective. Our purpose is two-fold: first to speak to the issues as contemporary demands upon Christian faith in hopes of giving guidance to persons who face these issues. Secondly, and this is a modest attempt, to provide a model for theological reflection on death and dying from the perspective of Christian theology.

The questions which I hear most frequently with regard to death in our contemporary society are these. Why does God allow good people to die tragic and untimely deaths? What happens to people who take their own lives – is suicide ever acceptable to God? Why cannot people be allowed to die a 'natural death' if their body is beyond healing and life must be sustained by artificial means? This last question is one which has special significance in light of recent technological developments in medical science. There are also important ethical considerations which we cannot ignore, but neither can we treat them fully in this discussion. These three questions raise issues to which we will now address our theological response.

'Tom' was a 30 year old man who left a successful career to come to my theological school to study for the Christian ministry. Six months after enrolling, he was suddenly taken to hospital with severe abdominal pain, and was diagnosed as having inoperable cancer of the liver. He was dead within six days. I visited him in hospital two days after his admission, when he had been told that he would die.

'Why would God let this happen to me,' he asked? 'If it is His will, then I can accept it. But for the first time in my life I thought I had a clear understanding of God's will for me, and I made my commitment to serve Him through the ministry of the Church. Was I wrong?'

Why does God allow good people to die tragic and untimely deaths? Tom was not claiming that he was too good to die, but he was asking for help in understanding how his death, at that particular time, and under those circumstances could be accepted as God's plan and will for his life.

One can fill in the name and particulars from other situations of which any one of us has some knowledge. Tom is not alone in asking this question. And yet he is alone, as is every person who faces his or her death suddenly, inexplicably, and without hope of surviving.

His Christian faith has raised the question to a more serious and profound level, rather than providing him with an answer. The distance between his body which was already a body of death and my body which did not know this with the same deadly certainty, was more than could be bridged by an embrace, much less the words of a theologian. How does one speak, above all how does one speak of God across that distance?

'A Christian in the state of grace dies a different death from that of the sinner', writes Karl Rahner.[5] I did not try to convince Tom of that. His death would be mean and vicious, with devastating physical and emotional pain. I did not attempt to defend that death in the name of God. This would be his own private holocaust and it must not be allowed to be identical with his history with God.

We agreed together that this deadly cancer had struck his body without regard to his being either in a secular occupation or studying in a theological school. We agreed that there is a history in which death works indiscriminately and without regard to its victims. Death knows nothing of the distinction between a person who is a sinner and one who is in a 'state of grace'.

But then we agreed also on the meaning of Christian faith as a participation of God in our history and of our participation in the history of death and resurrection of Jesus Christ. What he understood to be God's calling into Christian ministry was part of that time and history which bound his life into that of God. We talked about the fact that his life, from birth to death, had become part of that history of God which extends through death through Jesus Christ.

This, then, is what we believed concerning our life and what we could say about death. Thus the indiscriminate, brutal and senseless fact of death no longer stood over and against faith as an opponent and adversary, with its own power to destroy and deny the reality of life. Even as Jesus brought the terror of his own death within his relation to God as an affirmation of his life, so we too can bring our death, when it appears, within the relation we have to God in Christ.

In fairness to Rahner, this is surely what he meant when he said that the death of a Christian is different; but what is different is not the death, but the life of the Christian which enables faith to remain in continuity with God through the experience of death.

There is finally no comfort in a theological lecture. It is faith in the faithfulness of God which comforts and sustains life in the face of death. The business of theology is to assist faith in defining the substance of what is believed. But what is at stake in theological reflection upon the question of death is our apprehension of the very reality of God as the one whom we know in life.

It was the untimely and unfortunate death of his 14 year old son which caused Rabbi Harold Kushner to write his book *When Bad Things Happen to Good People*.[6] From the perspective of his traditional view of God as all powerful and also the source of all good, he found that he could no longer sustain theologically both concepts in light of the inexplicable suffering and death of his son. 'I can worship a God who hates suffering but cannot eliminate it,' he wrote, 'more easily than I can worship a God who chooses to make children suffer and die, for whatever exalted reason.'[7] He felt forced to the conclusion that if he had to choose between an all powerful God who would let his son suffer and die, or a God who was weak and not all powerful, but good and full of compassion for those who suffer, he would choose the latter. The question of death might seem to be a puzzle when experienced in old age, if one views the creation as the good work of God. One might attribute death to sin rather than to God, and so preserve the character of God. But when an innocent child (Kushner's son contracted the incurable disease at three years of age) is allowed to suffer and die by that same good creator, God, it does seem to question either the character or power of God.

I believe that the question can only be asked with regard to the power and goodness of God in the life, death and resurrection of his son, Jesus Christ. Kushner, being a modern Jew, is forced to identify God with the history of death. While this did not lead him to the death of God, as it has some, it did lead him to an 'impotent' but good God.

The theological reflections recorded in this book have led us to see our life and death as a continuum of history upon which occur random and indiscriminate events which have the power to 'take our life' in a physical sense. God's sovereignty and purpose cannot be located on this continuum as a cause and effect principle. Rather, God sovereignly and purposefully binds this life and death continuum of ours to the history of His own Son.

This is the perspective of the Apostle, who sees his own life as well as ours, securely placed within this Easter history of divine love and grace.

What then shall we say to this? If God is for us, who is against us? He who did not spare his own Son but gave him up for us all, will he not also give us all things with him? Who shall bring any charge against God's elect? It is God who justifies; who is to condemn? Is it Christ Jesus, who died, yes, who was raised from the dead, who is at the right hand of God, who indeed intercedes for us? Who shall separate us from the love of Christ? Shall tribulation, or distress, or persecution, or famine, or nakedness, or peril, or sword? ... No, in all these things we are more than conquerors through him who loved us. For I am sure that neither death, nor life, nor angels, nor principalities, nor things present, nor things to come, nor powers, nor height, nor depth, nor anything else in all creation, will be able to separate us from the love of God in Christ Jesus our Lord. (Romans 8:31–39)

Is it not significant that death is but one of the things which are comprehended in this list, and that life is one that is included? The entire spectrum of our human life, from birth to death is grasped by this comprehensive love of God in Christ. Not one thing which we can experience in our life time and within this cosmic order can slip out of this divine order of redemption.

We must then take this present history of ours with utmost seriousness, and not pick certain experiences to cherish as belonging to God and others left to float freely, unattached to His divine purpose for us. This will surely betray us in the end, if we do so. For we will see those very experiences which we cherish slip away from us, and those things which we fear the most close in on us relentlessly and inevitably.

But in taking our present life seriously, and not having contempt even for our own death, we do not surrender to this history of death an absolute power over us. Here is where God

displays His sovereignty and where He reveals Himself not to
be a crippled and impotent God. He is the God who encompasses our life and our death in such a way that He holds us fast
within the security and safety of the relation of Jesus Christ to
God his father. God's power and goodness are not played off
against each other in Jesus Christ. It was His goodness which
caused him to take upon himself our sicknesses and our death,
and it was His power which brought Christ, and so then us
with him, through death into eternal life.

This is what Tom and I agreed in faith and prayer. The
theological reflection follows faith and prayer, for the answer
must in this case precede the question. I could not answer
Tom's questions as a theologian. We discovered the answer as
Christians, together. The questions are left behind as exercises
for the theologian.

'John', on the other hand, was in excellent physical health
when he died. A successful engineer, and unmarried, he
struggled with loneliness and suffered through the breaking
up of an unsatisfactory relationship with a woman. He
appeared to find consolation in his relationship with God, but
then he was discovered dead in his car, with an open Bible
lying beside him. He had taken his own life.

As a pastor responsible for interpreting this death to the
survivors, I was challenged by a member of the Church for
providing a Christian funeral service: 'This man placed
himself outside of God's grace by taking his own life'.

Is this true? Is suicide different from other kinds of death? Is
death by one's own hand a death that is not included in the
saving death of Christ? What of a child who unknowingly
drinks a poisonous substance and subsequently dies? We are
told this is an accident, not a suicide, for though the death was
by the child's own hand it was not by the child's deliberate
intention.

So it seems it is not death itself, even death by one's own
hand, which places one outside of God's grace: it is the
intention which is the fatal sin. In this view, if suicide is not
only morally wrong but is a sin against God for which there is
no grace, then one surely is as guilty for an unsuccessful
suicide as a successful one. But then, so the argument runs,
one is granted a reprieve and so can repent and find grace from
God.

The fact that suicide is considered an unforgivable sin, in

this theological view, is based on a perspective of life which holds that one's relationship with God and one's existing in a state of grace is somehow dependent upon the fragile connection which is maintained by the individual's act of appropriating that grace. Dietrich Bonhoeffer, in his perceptive essay on suicide, strongly disagrees with this approach.[8]

Suicide is a specifically human act, says Bonhoeffer, because it issues out of the freedom which human beings possess. This freedom is not an absolute freedom and right over one's own life, to dispose of as one wishes, but is a freedom of life and death before God. The argument, widely used in the Christian church, that suicide rules out the possibility of repentance and therefore of forgiveness is invalid, Bonhoeffer argues. Many Christians have died without repenting of their sins. 'This is setting too much store by the last moment of life.'[9]

If suicide is to be declared wrong, says Bonhoeffer, and he agrees that it is, it cannot be decided before the forum of human morality but only before the forum of God. The freedom to die, which is given to natural life, is abused if it is used otherwise than in faith in God. The right to suicide is nullified only by the living God. Thus, Bonhoeffer continues, though despair may be the psychological condition which attends suicide in most cases, it cannot be counted as the originating cause. The originating cause of suicide is the freedom of the human person to act in self justification over and against God. Despair becomes the occasion for this act of self justification to take place.[10]

If we are to have a theological understanding of death through an intentional act of self destruction, we have been pointed in the right direction by Bonhoeffer's analysis. If, in fact, self justification, with its denial of the sovereignty of God over our life and death, is the basis for sin, rather than a last minute act of self destruction of the body, then we can ask the question within the act of God in Jesus Christ. It was, in fact, precisely because of the arrogance of self justification that human beings became sinners and came under the power of death. This self justification denies that our life is dependent upon God for its sustenance and survival. This 'deadly' condition produced by sin is present as the form of human life, afflicting all since Adam, according to Paul (cf. Romans 5:12–21).

The incarnation of God in Jesus Christ, taking this form of

death upon himself, turned the self justification of the sinner into the obedience of the Son, and through death, restored life to the disobedient. The death of one who commits suicide is *unnecessary* as a final desperate act of self justification. This is the tragedy in all such cases. Even the desperate act of Judas as an attempt to justify himself for his action of betrayal of Jesus was unnecessary. For the death of Jesus certainly was the end of all acts of self justification because it was the final death which sin itself produced.

Is it possible to say theologically that some acts of self justification which produce death are different from others, and that some which result in the ending of one's own physical life are somehow 'outside' of this act of God in Jesus Christ? Are there theological grounds to deny John the effects of the death and resurrection of Jesus *for sinners*? I think not. And yet, we cannot encourage or condone suicide in principle. If we no longer deny those who have taken their own lives burial in the 'sacred soil' of the churchyard, as was a former custom, neither can we ignore suicide as a serious social and human problem. There *is* something terribly wrong when self inflicted death is a better solution than life for so many people.

Of course, suicide is viewed quite differently in other cultures and other times. In the Graeco-Roman world, we are told that no stigma was attached, though the practice was not so common as in certain eastern and Asian societies.[11] Our western society, with a strong influence from the Judaeo-Christian tradition, has generally viewed suicide as a *felo de se*, or as a crime against oneself. In fact, in Britain it was considered a crime up to the passing of the Suicide Act of 1961. Even under this law, it remains an offence to assist a suicide. In the United States, suicide is still a crime in several states.

With over 25,000 suicides reported each year in the United States, with estimates that the actual number is at least double that, and with attempted suicides numbering more than 100,000 each year, the statistics are alarming. Recent British studies show that nearly 10 out of every 1,000 admissions at hospital emergency departments are due to self poisoning, a prevalence rate of 430 per 100,000 of the population. This means that over the course of just one year, 1 person out of every 230 of the adult population of London attempts suicide by means of poison.[12]

Every idea of death is a version of life, it was stated at the outset of this chapter. Suicide reflects a version of life held by a significant number of our society. If Bonhoeffer was right when he said the right to suicide is nullified only by the living God, this is properly a theological concern, and not merely a sign of despair. Nor can one accept these statistics and the increasing prevalence of suicide as a sign that modern people are assuming, rightfully, control over their own lives. We cannot support the contention that human dignity and 'self ownership' are universal values belonging to each individual.[13]

By definition, Christian theology asserts that human persons as created in the image and likeness of God have dignity and value in terms of relatedness to God and to each other. The claim to dignity and the right over one's own life in an absolute sense is a denial of this dignity and value as constituted by our being created in God's image. To claim this as an individual right is an act of self justification, to use Bonhoeffer's language. If we grant the right to commit suicide, we are denying for ourselves a fundamental element in our own humanity. The theological case against suicide must be a case for the integrity of human life as co-responsibility. The one who commits suicide tears something from the fabric of human life itself when he departs.

'John', who died at his own hands, with an open Bible beside him, could not feel this co-responsibility as an essentially valuable part of his own human life, but we can and do and this is why there are theological grounds for saying that John's act against his own humanity cannot overturn the act of God in Jesus Christ for humanity, and indeed for John.

Let us consider another case. Elizabeth Bouvia had death on her mind when she checked in to a hospital in Riverside, California in September 1983. Although suffering from the crippling effects of cerebral palsy since birth, she had, none the less earned a bachelor's degree in social work, and had even attempted a marriage relationship. But at the age of 26, and confined to a wheelchair, suffering from painful arthritis and unable even to feed herself, she had concluded that life under these conditions was intolerable. She checked in to hospital for the clearly stated purpose of dying through starvation. Her request was that the hospital staff provide minimal hygienic care and reduce whatever pain she would have while she died.

She planned to 'refuse further nutrients and permit the natural process of dying to occur'.[14]

The staff refused to cooperate with her wishes, and she was force-fed a liquid diet in order to prevent her death. Her situation attracted the attention of the Hemlock Society, a group committed to legalizing the right to suicide, who argued that she had the right to determine, with dignity, her own time and means of death.

Elizabeth did not die, as she had hoped. She finally accepted the reality of her situation, took solid food and was discharged under the care of others. The legal implications were quite clear. Under the law, any one who became an accomplice of her volitional death could be prosecuted.

The theological implications are not so easy to see. The issue becomes one of quality of life. At what point does human life, even when viewed as co-responsibility, become so distorted and without value that death actually is more 'appropriate' than life? If the task of life includes that of embracing one's suffering in a meaningful way, can that task be expected of others whether they want it or not? Or is that something that each one of us must decide for ourselves?

Questions crowd upon us. If Elizabeth should ask me to justify the fact that she is expected to continue to live with pain and humiliation, can I do that as a way of pointing out God's will for her? What threshold of suffering is there in human pain that will permit us to say – in the name of God – enough?

Surely this is the wrong way to get at a theological perspective in this case. The attempt to draw a distinction between 'good' suffering and 'bad suffering' is not valid. We *can* coach each other on finding access to the resources that will permit us to summon courage and faith from within ourselves. The grace and power of God is such a resource; and it is a travesty of God's grace to link it to an imperative which seeks to turn bad suffering into good suffering.

There are some who argue, theologically, that each person's life is providentially determined by God, and that to cut short the precise 'number of days' that God has allowed one to live is presumption against God's providence. From this view comes the often heard charge that to allow life to be terminated is to 'play God'.

One could well understand that this view could serve at a

time when death could not be prevented, or extended. But now that the time of death can be extended, in some cases for long periods, with no evidence of personal consciousness, the presumption against providence works the other way. To force life to be extended beyond 'natural death' could be viewed as violating God's providence.

Avery Weisman has suggested that we remember the Greek concept of time as *kairos* – an auspicious moment that leads to a decisive change. Thus, he suggests that death may be viewed as 'appropriate' in certain cases. That is, that it is acceptable because it is the right 'time'. In this sense, death is 'appropriated' through a purposeful decision to end physical life, under conditions which are appropriate.[15] The appropriate conditions include an optimum reduction of pain and suffering, and the willingness to yield control to others in whom one has confidence. Weisman acknowledges that these conditions are idealistic and not likely to occur for most people.

This raises the theological question, however, of the concept of a 'good death', or of euthanasia, as it is usually spoken of. In 1974, The General Synod Board for Social Responsibility of the Church of England issued a report entitled *On Dying Well*. The report attempted to continue the use of the concept of euthanasia, while qualifying some of the pejorative connotations which the term has acquired.[16]

'The individual is conceived to enjoy, in some sense, a right to die', the report asserted. While not justifying mercy killing or suicide, the report does attempt to place the event of dying in a context of human care and scientific knowledge. Theologically, the report saw death as an event which has a Godward dimension as well as a manward and natural dimension. This leads the report to resist approving or permitting any form of voluntary euthanasia as a 'breach of moral wisdom'. The report stops short of defining the role of the Christian community in deciding when death is appropriate and thus can be 'appropriated,' to use Weisman's term.

Helmut Thielicke argues that persons have a 'right to die' as a function of the dignity of life which God has given. Choosing to avoid the term, euthanasia, he suggests, instead, the term 'orthothanasia' – right dying.[17] To refuse to take heroic measures is not to violate human dignity, Thielicke argues, for human dignity is not located essentially in the biological aspect of life, but in the human person as a God-given endowment of life.

Take another case. One Sunday afternoon, a father called me to come to the hospital where 'Gary' lay in a coma. He was four years old, and had been struck by a car. His father, who was also a medical doctor, had attended him for the past 36 hours since the accident, monitoring his vital signs. His skull had been crushed, and he was kept alive only by the respirator to which he was attached.

The father said he would take one more EEG reading and if there were no signs of brain activity, he wanted to disconnect the respirator and let the boy die. 'We can keep his body functioning for a few more days, and possibly longer,' he said, 'but I believe that we should release him to be with God if that is his will.'

Here the father was not really asking for my opinion as a pastor and a theologian, he was seeking confirmation of what we both believed about the nature of human personhood. To allow a person to die, even a four year old, he believed would not be the end of his life, but the continuation of it with God through the power of the resurrection of Jesus Christ. In prayer and faith we agreed that extraordinary measures to prolong the mechanical functions of breathing were beyond the definition of human life as more than sheer biological existence, and so the machine was disconnected.

In the past few years, legal and ethical issues have arisen which would make impossible, or at the least, extremely difficult, the decision which we made on behalf of Gary. I am not so sure that this has been to our advantage or to the advantage of the dying.

What is feared, of course, is that decisions will be made in situations like this which encroach upon the right to life of the dying person himself or herself. But the act of sustaining biological life through artificial means is also a decision. To allow the decision to extend biological life, and to permit the definition of clinical death to be made primarily in terms of scientific or technological criteria may itself be an act of irresponsibility, humanly and theologically speaking.

At this point, the restrictions we would want to place upon those who assume an arbitrary authority over extending life issue from the same theological grounds as restrictions we would want to place on the right to commit suicide.

Christian theology cannot support suicide as an individual's right over his or her own life because it violates the fundamental co-responsibility for life which constitutes human personhood. Such an act of self destruction tears the fabric of life out of our hands. For the same reason, many Christians reject the concept of an absolute right to extend biological life through extraordinary means. This cannot be justified in the name of life, because it too, in the extreme, can tear the fabric of human life out of our hands, and violate the fundamental co-responsibility which upholds the integrity and sanctity of life.

A Christian perspective on death is grounded in the tension that must be maintained between support of physical life through all means possible and, at the same time, the appropriateness of death when human life is itself in danger of becoming grotesque and even monstrous. 'We are forbidden to hamper the Lord of life and death by medical gadgetry that can also lead to madness,' writes Thielicke.[18]

Determining the point where this 'madness' occurs, of course, is the critical issue. It certainly is not a theological decision alone. But the context in which this decision is made must include, in addition to scientific experts, an authentic community with a theological perspective on human life. This perspective includes an eschatological point of view, in which life and death are viewed as already held fast within God's actions in Jesus Christ.

This eschatological perspective on life clarifies the subtle distinction between human nature as 'bios' and human life as 'zoe'. Quality of life cannot be determined solely by extending the biological life of human persons. The concept of life as revealed in the New Testament, particularly in light of the life which issues from Jesus Christ, is participation in the life of God which is given to human persons by creation and extended through death by the redemption and life (zoe) of Christ. In the gospel of John, in particular, as well in the Synoptics and the Pauline letters, 'zoe' refers to a person's life made abundantly full, and this life is inseparable from Jesus Christ as the source of life (cf. John 10:10; 1 Tim. 6:11, 12, 19). Thus, instead of bioethics as an approach to the crucial life and death decision about which we have been speaking, Professor Robert Nelson suggests that we think of 'zoethics'.[19]

We have argued that this theological perspective is rooted in

the Christian belief that human life and death are bracketed
under the determination of God. We have shown that the life,
death and resurrection of Jesus Christ has enfolded the life and
death of human persons within that eschatological time and
history which Easter reveals.

The deaths of children, the untimely and unfortunate deaths
of the healthy, the tragic and unnecessary death by suicide, the
slow and bewildering death of the terminally ill, as well as the
death which seems finally to be 'appropriate', these deaths are
all of a kind, despite the circumstances which attend each.
Some of these deaths cause anger and consternation; some
result in a grief which life itself cannot ever dissolve; some
appear as a blessed end to a full life. But a Christian
perspective on death cannot make one death more acceptable
than another, nor set any death outside of the death and
resurrection of Jesus Christ.

A Christian perspective on dying is really a version of life. It
is living and dying in the light shed by the resurrection of
Christ. This does not make dying any less difficult, but it
brings it within the grasp of our humanity. We owe one
another a human context for dying.

NOTES

1 Avery D. Weisman, 'Appropriate and Appropriated Death', in *Death: Current Perspectives*, edited by Edwin S. Shneidman (Palo Alto, CA: Mayfield Publishing, 1976), p. 502.
2 *Church Dogmatics* (Edinburgh: T. & T. Clark, 1960), volume 3, part 2, p. 348.
3 *The Way of Torah: An Introduction to Judaism* p. 56. Cited by James Carse, *Death and Existence* (New York: Wiley, 1980), p. 211.
4 *God's Presence in History*, p. 84. Cited in Carse, *Death and Existence*, p. 212.
5 *On the Theology of Death* (New York: Herder and Herder, 1967), p. 67.
6 Harold S. Kushner, *When Bad Things Happen to Good People* (New York: Avon Books, 1981).
7 Ibid., p. 134.
8 *Ethics* (New York: Macmillan, 1955), pp. 166–72.
9 Ibid., p. 169.
10 Ibid., pp. 167, 168. Paul Tillich also argues that suicide should not be singled out for exceptional moral condemnation. He does feel that suicide is caused by despair, but responds by saying that suicide is not a good option because one cannot 'escape' despair through suicide. Despair can only be overcome through eternity, and eternity is accessible only through existence, not non-existence; *Systematic Theology* (Chicago: University of Chicago Press, 1957), volume 2, pp. 76ff.
11 For a discussion of suicide in various cultures, see *Death: Current Perspectives*, pp. 16–18. For statistics concerning suicidal deaths and the factors which seem to contribute to suicides, see *The Facts of Death* (Englewood Cliffs, NJ: Prentice-Hall, 1979), by Michael Simpson, pp. 202–21.
12 Cited by Simpson, *The Facts of Death*, pp. 202–3.
13 H. Thielicke makes this same point in *Living With Death* (Grand Rapids: Eerdmans, 1983), pp. 75ff.
14 Source, *Los Angeles Times*, 30 November 1983, Part V. See also *Time Magazine*, 14 November 1983.
15 'Appropriate and Appropriated Death', in *Death: Current Perspectives*, pp. 502–6.
16 Cited in *Will to Live/Will to Die* (Minneapolis: Augsburg, 1978), by Kenneth Vaux, pp. 95ff.
17 *Living With Death*, pp. 79–80.
18 Ibid., pp. 81–2.
19 *Human Life – A Biblical Perspective for Bioethics* (Philadelphia:

Fortress Press, 1984), pp. 107ff. Nelson's book is a rich resource of theological and ethical wisdom with regard to a Christian perspective on human life as a context for examining issues related to human death.

CHAPTER 8

The Human Ecology of Death and Dying

My father died at home, in his own bed. The cancer which relentlessly destroyed body tissue finally caused him to slip into a coma. The physician made an occasional visit to the house, but his dying, like his birth, was domestic and familial. There were no tubes linking him to an artificial source of life, nor were there electronic screens flickering and beeping with his vital life signs.

My hand on his chest felt the last few shuddering beats of the heart, and he was dead, but he was still father, husband, brother to those around him.

His sister took his false teeth out of the glass, adjusted them in his mouth and closed it. Taking a towel, she wrapped it around his chin and forehead, restoring his familiar face. And suddenly his humanity was healed, as though she were recreating him again out of the lump of clay that God originally wrought into a human being. Asking for two coins, she closed his eyes, gently, placing them on his eyelids to keep them closed. I was a silent participant in an ancient ritual that knew instinctively and certainly what it was doing. Something deep inside of me knew that this was good, and that one generation was preparing another to embrace and uphold this mystery.

This scene could hardly take place today. We know too much about how to keep death from having its way quickly. But this knowledge is not carried in the wisdom of the family; it is the secret of science and its mysteries lie behind closed doors where masked faces peer impersonally at the flow of data which tell more than the hand upon the chest.

Dying is a last resort, when all else fails. But in our modern era the failure of family to keep the dying within its boundaries is nowhere near the last failure.

It is for the sake of preserving life that the family is forced to abandon its members to the technical and professional supervision of the healers. But with this transfer of authority, there is also a transfer from one environment into another. It is not just that physicians no longer make house calls out of the need for more efficient deployment of their time. The environment, or culture of healing, has become a new technological womb. Here too there is an umbilical cord which connects both patient and healer to a 'third force' which powers up the life-preserving apparatus.

Here too, of course, there is finally failure. Here is the place of last resort. The survivors are now 'informed', and the process of grieving and disposal begins.

This 'modernization' of dying was, of course, not planned. It is the result of incredible advances in the science of medicine and surgical procedures. Over and against what has been said above must be placed the stories of those who have survived what, in the past, would have been certain death if left in the environment of the family. No parent today will conclude that a child who has been pulled from a swimming pool unconscious is yet dead. Instead, the emergency services are called, and the child is rushed to hospital, where, in many cases, life is restored.

Even where death seems inevitable because the disease has been pronounced incurable, the process of dying is often too painful and the task of providing the necessary physical care too demanding for family members to cope.

Hospitals are not only places for healing, they are also places for dying. Both health care and dying care are a result of the modernization of medicine, and both can contribute to the humanization or the dehumanization of life.

What has not received appropriate recognition in this modern process of healing and dying, is the human environment which may also be an important factor. This is of theological concern because it is fundamentally a human concern and a concern for the dignity of human personhood through the experience of death. Human personhood is defined theologically in terms of the image and likeness of God as expressed through relationships. Dying moves the individual more and more towards isolation. Dying is a solitary experience. The network of human relationships which sustains personhood during life must also provide the environment of personhood through dying.

In a series of papers published under the title of *Death, Dying and Disposal*, there is an essay on 'Architecture for Mourning' and one also on 'The Environment of Disposal'.[1] What is missing is any treatment of the human environment of dying itself. It is this environment, or culture, which I attempted to capture in the telling of the story of the death of my father.

It is clear that the human environment of dying was itself a casualty of the modernization of medicine and health care. We cannot go back, ever again, to that earlier state of the art where the limits of life preservation were reached without breaking out of the boundaries of family love and care. The humanization of dying must not be viewed as an attempt to sentimentalize dying; nor should our concern for the recovery of the human environment of dying be motivated by nostalgia.

No more can we be content with reviewing the literature on counselling the dying and the grieving. The greater share of the literature on dying produced in the past 25 years has to do with the psychological and therapeutic aspects of dying and grieving. This is also true for the literature on pastoral care of the dying. The impressive annotated bibliography on death and dying produced by Leonard Pearson includes over 650 titles, and is already more than a decade out of date.[2] In the interim the important work of Elizabeth Kübler-Ross has been published, along with a host of other books which deal with death and dying from a psychological and therapeutic perspective.[3]

Without diminishing the value and importance of the psychological and therapeutic issues which relate to death and dying, it is my intention to focus more specifically upon a theological concern for the human factor in death and dying.

The word 'ecology' is a helpful one which directs our attention to the interconnection that exists between the biological function of an organism and its environment. The human ecology of death and dying, as a theme for this chapter, suggests that death is more than a biological act in which a person perishes as an organism. Rather, because the human person is human by virtue of relatedness to other humans, as well as to God, there is an ecological factor which also affects the human person as an organism.

This has been noted most recently in the process of giving birth. Delivery rooms in some hospitals have been modified to provide more of a domestic environment, with not only the architecture and interior design thus 'humanized', but where participation of family members in the event is encouraged. The ecological factor of the infant's arrival in the world in this setting of direct exposure to human touch and familial love and care is thought to be beneficial to the baby's needs as an organism as well as to future personality development. The fundamentally human event of birth also contributes to the humanity and personal life of those who experience it: the ecological factor works both ways.

In the same way, there is now a movement to 'humanize' the event of dying through providing a more domestic and familial type of caring environment. Experiments in pain control have shown that injections accompanied by prayer and the touching of the person's body are more effective than when performed as a routine medical procedure.[4] Pain is not merely a biological phenomenon, it is a factor of human ecology as well. Pain may not only have psychosomatic factors, but sociosomatic ones as well. The ecology of death leads us to acknowledge a many-faceted network of relations to which the dying person is connected. Not least of which is the relation of the person to God.

During the last few hours of my father's life, when he had been completely unresponsive to verbal communication and physical touch by family members for some time, his pastor called at the house. Moving to the side of the bed on which my father lay, the pastor began to read the 23rd Psalm. My father immediately brought his hands up from his side and folded them on his breast. No other movement or response was made, except this response to hearing the Word of God. There is a spiritual ecology of death and dying as well.

Certainly the most remarkable and encouraging sign of the development of a human ecology of death and dying is the hospice movement. The Latin word *hospes* meant both host and guest. The word connotes an interaction between human persons, not merely a physical environment, or a 'place to stay'.

The Latin word, of course, has evolved into a variety of contemporary expressions, among them the words 'hostel', 'hotel', 'hospital' and 'hospice'.

Strangely, the hospital has now become a place noted for its neutralizing effect upon personal and human interactions. 'Hospital makes war, not love', writes Sandol Stoddard, in her definitive work on the hospice movement.[5]

According to Stoddard, the medieval *hospice* was in operation throughout Europe, including England, as a place which provided an open door to the sick and dying, but also to the hungry and the wayfarer, to the woman in labour, the needy poor and the orphan. The common denominator was 'hospitality'. While the medicine was primitive and 'home grown', using herbs and other ointments, the ecological factor of human care and human relationships was the principle offering.[6]

The modern hospice movement, with a focused care for dying persons, had its clearest beginning with the founding of St Christopher's Hospice in London. Dr. Cicely Saunders, founder and director, traces the antecedents of the modern hospice back to the medieval hospices, but more recently to Mother Mary Aidenhead, who used the concept of hospice when she founded the Irish Sisters of Charity in the middle of the nineteenth century. Yet, as Dr Saunders reports, the Hospice at Harold's Cross, Dublin, dedicated especially to dying patients, was only founded at the turn of the twentieth century.[7] Dr Saunder's work at St Christopher's began in 1967, and since that time, the hospice movement has developed in England and has spread to the United States.

The hospice, says Sandol Stoddard, is an idea whose time has come. Seeking to retrieve what has been most humane and sensible in the tradition of healing and ministry to the dying, the hospice seeks to establish a new standard for care of the sick and dying without diminishing the effective resources of medical science. The key word for the hospice is 'community'.

At the centre of the hospice community is the concept of 'a body coexisting with a belief'.[8] The body is the dying patient, and the belief is that the patient is something more than a body.

The hospice movement recognizes that specialized care is necessary for dying persons, and that the home and family unit cannot always provide that. Yet, the network of caring human beings as the environment of the dying person can be provided through the people who staff the hospice as well as through trained staff and volunteers who regularly visit dying people in their own home environment.

A 'hospice person', then, is one who knows that contact with the living is contact with life which is already in the process of dying. Yet this person also knows that for the living to remain in community with the dying is also essential to the true value of a human life and community.[9] The hospice community embraces patient, family and close friends, says Sandol Stoddard, 'not only during the final days and weeks of the patient's life, but long after death, offering consolation and support during the time of bereavement.'[10]

The hospice is not first of all an institution, but it is a community in need of a home. The establishment of inpatient facilities creates a surrogate home and offers a context of community for the patient. This facility is not a 'fortress' separated from the rest of society, but a 'house of life', a place where dying can be experienced as part of the human pilgrimage.[11] Many hospices, modelled after St Christopher's in London, have also become teaching communities where volunteers who already are 'hospice persons' learn how to create this community through home visitation. We cannot assume that the typical family today knows how to integrate the dying person into the domestic life of the family, and how to create a caring community which includes the dying.

I have pointed to the development of the hospice movement as a sign of the recovery of an authentic human ecology of death and dying. I believe this movement has instincts that are grounded in a view of human personhood which anticipates our theological concern for a perspective on death and dying which is genuinely Christian.

What specifically then is meant by a human ecology for death and dying? It means, of course, the fact that human life is a co-responsibility which includes the death of one another as part of that mutuality of concern. Several things can be listed as belonging to this co-responsibility for upholding one another in death.

We uphold the humanity of the other when that person no longer has control of his or her own human environment. The dignity of personhood is precarious and subject to many indignities. We tolerate these indignities when they are temporary and when we are sure that we will soon have control of our own personal space and bodily functions again. A visit to the dentist for even a routine check up is a brief surrender of our bodily privacy. The invasion of the body through a physical examination by a surgeon is a humiliation of a higher degree which we accept as long as we recover!

What happens in the process of dying and at the moment of death is not merely an intensification of these experiences. There is a qualitative difference in that the surrender of personal control over one's own body and private space is at some point permanent. When this is marked by the transfer of our body out of the familiar space of our own domestic and familial life, we are bound to experience ecological shock. The fact that this is meant for our good, and that the body can now receive care that will ensure its survival for a longer period of time, is often taken as both necessary and good.

What may not be recognized is that what we define as the essential humanity of personal existence is not identical with the prolongation of bodily existence. Not only that, but under the neutralizing conditions of medical care as experienced in many modern hospitals, the ecological system which is necessary for the upholding of our human dignity can be broken.

This is reflected in the 'rush to disposal' which often follows immediately upon the medical pronouncement of death. Moreover this pronouncement must now be given by the professional. No longer can we assume the responsibility for pronouncing one who belongs to us as now dead. Within a few minutes, usually, the bereaved are separated from the deceased. Disposal of the body is handed over to other professionals, and the grief counselling turned over to the religious professionals. The family system as a social and ecological network, unfortunately, is not often considered to have expertise in dealing with death nor with grief.

Why are we sure that personhood is dissolved so precisely at the point of clinical death? From a theological perspective, certainly, we understand that there is a point where the body of a human person becomes a corpse. But there are also theological grounds for suggesting that this point cannot be determined clinically with absolute precision. This 'decision' as to when we should turn away from the body and view it now as a corpse is itself part of the human ecology of personhood, and not merely a unit of information on an electronic screen.

An argument can be made for the presence of the human network which upholds the dignity and humanity of the person even through that ambiguous point of death. The decision, then, ought to include the information provided by medical science, but not be identical with it.

The physician was called, and did render his medical decision with regard to the death of my father. But his decision was a certification of death on the only grounds of which he was capable – biological evidence. This decision was not questioned, but it was not allowed to be a decision that severed immediately the ecological network of which my father was a part as a member of the human family. The actual decision by which his death is acknowledged and affirmed by this human family is itself a process, a ritual, if you like, of the community itself.

Those brief moments following death, when the body of a loved person is attended by those who are yet responsible for the humanity of the person, are not capitulations to mere sentiment and maudlin grief. The moment of death is the moment of absolute vulnerability of the person who dies. The authority and control over one's own personal existence in bodily form is surrendered irrevocably. The tenuous, and yet intimate connection between the self and the body is now dissolved. The ecology of the person as an embodied self, as a human person, is suspended in the continued relation which is affirmed from the side of the living.

This is a time of transition from one form of personal existence to another. Christian theology affirms that this transition is upheld by the power of God's love in Jesus Christ, and that with the Apostle, one can say that to depart this body is to 'be with Christ' (Philippians 1:23). But this departure, is itself, a human event, not a spiritual retreat from reality. This is to say, let my body go when I die, for it has been taken from the dust and to the dust it will return; but stand with me and my body as it is returned to this good earth.

It is a fallacy to assume that this process is only a bit of folklore, to be viewed merely as a quaint custom which no longer has relevance with the advent of more sophisticated and precise standards of determining death. The argument is not for a return to a certain custom, but for a recovery of the process by which human persons are upheld as such through the time of their death.

This is a theological argument for the right to challenge the pre-emptory right of professional medical science to exclude the family from the process of determining death and from the ritual of preparing the body for disposal. It will be said in response that our modern society does not wish to be involved in this process, and that we are not psychologically prepared to undertake this task. Perhaps not but then this is too great a concession to the secularization of life and death itself. The Christian community, at the very least, should be prepared through instruction and encouragement to recover the human ecology of death and dying as a matter of its own theological integrity.

Christians, one is sorry to say, may be among the least prepared to provide this 'hospice' for its own members. Is this because the Church tends to concentrate on preparing its members for the heavenly pleasures of the next life rather than on the serious business of upholding the humanity of one's life and death in this life? Or is this merely another example of the ease with which the Church accepts the secularization of human life as a convenience?

Whatever the reason, there is no basis for this failure on theological grounds, not to mention what the instincts of authentic humanity tell us.

I have set out one aspect of a human ecology in death and dying – the responsibility to uphold the human dignity of the other in the process of dying. The theological mandate is that we can and must find ways to recover the authority to release a member of our human community at death by insisting that medical care of the dying and medical certification of death take place, in so far as possible, within the ecological system of human family and community.

A second aspect of a human ecology viewed as co-responsibility is that of upholding the truthfulness of death through the process of dying. This means that the ultimate betrayal of personhood is to deceive another about his or her death. 'There is no escaping the difficult question whether we do not owe the truth to the mortally sick,' says Helmut Thielicke.[12] It is a difficult question because the truth of death is not a simple fact, and it cannot be simply told. We must 'speak the truth in love', urges Paul (Ephesians 4:15).

There are several reasons why the dying might be spared knowledge of their impending death. Physicians are responsible for the general well-being of their patients, and the emotional shock of being told of one's imminent death may upset the delicate balance of the patient's condition. Some are even prepared to say that 'there are lies which express profound human love'.[13] Telling the truth may cause unnecessary pain and even undermine the physical condition of the patient, some have argued.

The diagnosis of death is difficult to determine. Even a so-called incurable disease is, at best, a judgement based on current medical opinion. There remain many factors that could make the diagnosis wrong, or at least qualify it. For this reason, medical doctors are often reluctant to tell a patient that death is a likely outcome.

There may be a deeper reason for concealing death and maintaining silence concerning it in talking with dying persons. The therapeutic and existential value of hope is a powerful life force. The truth itself may have a fatal effect upon this life force. Not many persons can sustain hope and a will to live when confronted with their inevitable death.

But what happens to the ecology of personal existence as co-responsibility when death remains a silent secret in the relation? Awareness of death is also a fundamental aspect of the 'truth of life'. To be overtaken by death, as a sudden and unanticipated intruder, is to have lived a lie. It is, indeed, a difficult question.

Quite clearly, the reasons cited above for concealing the fact of death are not really arguments against the truth, but are warnings that this truth cannot easily be told. It can only be lived and learned.

Thielicke reminds us of the difficulty of speaking of truth by suggesting that a teenager writing in a school essay that 'Goethe is the greatest German poet', has made a correct statement. Yet, on his inexperienced lips, it is more of a fraud than a truth. Truth, as more than a fact, must be brought to light through a process of personal experience. In this case, we have a truth at the wrong time, which is consequently no truth at all.[14]

The dying are not usually without knowledge of death. Often this is experienced as a repressed knowledge. Here then we are dealing with a truth which is known but not acknowledged. To remain silent is to participate in this conspiracy against truth which separates a person from his or her own inner truth of being. In this case, the truth needs to be 'released' in a Socratic sense.

We return to our theme of a human ecology for death and dying as a theological theme of 'being in the truth' as a form of human relationship and community. This can be expressed in more technical language by saying that there is an ontological depth of personhood by which the truth of life and death can be experienced. Being in human relationship, with a relationship with God also presumed through faith and experience, our very being is conditioned by the truth of our mortality. We uphold each other, not by concealing this ontological truth, and participating in a conspiracy against our very being, but by bringing this truth within the reality of our personal existence.

Rather than the truth of dying constituting a shock to the person, it can actually be a therapeutic gain and a resource of courage and hope. Concealment of the reality of dying skates upon the superficial psychological surface of our lives. Hope and courage which are only the result of freedom from psychological anxiety are not yet a deep and powerful human hope and courage.

The question of whether or not a dying person should be told the truth, is finally the question: 'Who am I with regard to this person? What do we know together of the truth of life and death? Am I able to discover this truth of death in my partner, my friend, my neighbour, as *our* truth?'

So yes, it is correct to say that we all, some day, will die. But we prepare for the truth of that experience when we have created a life in community with those who will not conceal the truth from us at the very last.

I have made two points about what it means to uphold each other in co-responsibility through death. We must uphold the dignity of the person and we must uphold the truth of the person through the experience of dying and death. I have alluded to a third point, and that is to uphold the faith of a person who is dying.

Our perspective, after all, is one provided by a Christian

theology of death and dying. This does not mean that we are only concerned with the death of those who profess Christian faith. Rather, we approach dying and death from the perspective of the reality we confess by faith – that Jesus Christ took to himself the span of human life and death, and that he was raised from the dead. This reality of the incarnation, death and resurrection of Jesus Christ is the new humanity upon which all humanity now rests as its ultimate basis. This is what faith believes when it is Christian faith.

But the very nature of Christian faith is that this reality is an ultimate reality; it is not yet a consummated and completed reality for us which is why it is a reality that is upheld by faith.

The word which faith believes concerning our life and death is the ultimate or last word. This word has been revealed to us through the resurrection of Jesus Christ, as the testimony of his witnesses and the Holy Spirit. Yet, we live in the next to last, or penultimate time. In this penultimate time, life and death continue to demand of us serious attention. Our humanity is spiritually orientated to the new humanity which we share with Christ, but this spiritual orientation does not evacuate the present, or penultimate time of its reality and meaning.

The promises which we hold by faith concerning a new humanity, where death is removed and where there will be no more pain and tears, no more sorrow and suffering, these promises give substance to our faith; they are not meant to be the bread we eat, the water we drink, nor the medicine we take when we are sick. Nor are these promises of ultimate health and eternal life given to us so that we might despise the penultimate life, with its sorrows and sicknesses.

This Christian perspective is not easy to sustain. Some lose sight of the promises altogether and sink into the present reality with a fatalism and despair which concedes all hope to the inevitable victory of sickness and death. Others grasp at the promises with spiritual and emotional fanaticism, living on the precarious edge of the miraculous and the fantastic.

The early Christians moved into the world with a message that Jesus Christ is Lord of life and death, and that salvation and healing has come to all people through his death and resurrection. Their witness to this reality was accompanied by 'signs and wonders', as Luke records the ministry of those early

Apostles (Acts 4:29–30). The sick were often healed, demons were cast out, even the dead were raised. The early Church viewed these phenomena as signs which attested to the reality and power of the gospel. The scripture reminds Christians to pray for the sick, and to provide hospitality for the poor and homeless, as evidences of the reality of Christ in this present world (cf. James 5:13–16; 1 John 3:17–18; Hebrews 13:1–3).

The injunction to pray for the healing of the sick has caused more difficulty, strangely enough, than the command to practise hospitality and care for the poor. Prayer for the sick has often been interpreted as the appropriation of a promise given through the death and resurrection of Christ. The answer to this prayer, in the view of some, is a supernatural act of healing by which the natural process of sickness and death is reversed, at least for a time. The command to provide hospitality and care for the poor and hungry does not seem to commend the same interest and fascination. The promise concerning prayer for the sick fascinates but also perplexes, because we do not always know what it means to pray.

Some have interpreted this promise to mean that every person has a right to expect that God will heal the one who prays in faith. Stories of such apparently miraculous healings are used to support this expectation. This poses a problem: how do we uphold the faith of the dying person in light of these promises and these expectations? How do I pray for the healing of the person who is dying and remain *truthful* to the reality of death?

I make this suggestion. Praying for the sick may be understood as 'preparing the way of the Lord'. Rightly understood, prayer is not a means by which God is invoked to deliver a solution to our need or to give us an advantage over the mortality of others. Rather, prayer appropriates us to the promise of God which has been fulfilled in Jesus Christ and will be fulfilled in our own release from the power of death. 'Prayer', writes Jacques Ellul, 'is the crossing of a boundary, it is the means of making a lawful entrance into the closed world. . . Prayer holds together the shattered fragments of the creation. It makes history possible. Therefore it is the victory over nothingness.'[15]

Prayer, then, is preparing the way of the Lord. It is the preparing of the way through our own lives for his glorious victory to be completed. Thus, prayer for the one who is sick and dying is not a desperate and fanatical act to gain a supernatural intervention as an advantage over life, with its sickness and death. Rather, it is the appropriation of one's life into the ultimate healing event, which takes place through death and resurrection.

Where there are evidently manifestations of immediate healing as an answer to prayer, these healings are to be viewed as a 'sacrament' of the resurrection itself, and a sign to the entire community that the promise of ultimate healing is true. Therefore, the healing of one person is not a 'truth' which condemns others who are not healed. The healing of the one is a sacrament of that truth which holds good for all. Healing is a gift of God to the community for the purpose of sustaining the faith of the members of the community.

The confusion of the ultimate with the penultimate, to use Dietrich Bonhoeffer's helpful distinction, is a cause of many difficulties in this area. The resurrection of Christ, says Bonhoeffer, does not annul the penultimate, 'but the eternal life, the new life, breaks in with ever greater power into the earthly life and wins its space for itself within it.'[16] This space is not a privileged space for the Christian, with freedom from the realities of this world and mortal life. The space is the sphere of Christian faith lived out in the world as the presence of the ultimate reality in the very midst of the penultimate. This is why, Bonhoeffer goes on to say,

> in thoroughly grave situations, for instance when I am with someone who has suffered a bereavement, I often decide to adopt a 'penultimate' attitude, ... remaining silent as a sign that I share in the bereaved man's helplessness in the face of such a grievous event, and not speaking the biblical words of comfort which are, in fact, known to me and available to me. Why am I often unable to open my mouth, when I ought to give expression to the ultimate? And why, instead, do I decide on an expression of thoroughly penultimate human solidarity?[17]

Bonhoeffer is not proposing silence in the face of suffering and bereavement, but a reluctance to violate the integrity of the present time for the sake of a speech about the ultimate realities. Prayer for the sick is a way of preparing for the way of the Lord in our lives, without breaking that necessary and appropriate 'silence' concerning ultimate things. The very solidarity which one has with the dying person is a form of the presence of the ultimate reality itself, and one ought not to break this bond of human fellowship by resorting to the miraculous as the sole sign of divine presence and healing.

There is a human ecology which upholds our human dignity, the truth of our human life and death, and the faith by which we live with hope and courage. Faith is difficult to sustain through 'prevailing fever'. There is an ecology of faith as well. There is a 'hospice' for Christian faith; it is the community of those who uphold the truth and promise of baptism on our behalf when we are too ignorant or too weak or too confused to call ourselves 'child of God'. This 'hospice of Christian community' enfolds us through the eucharistic celebration of forgiveness, healing and hope in Jesus Christ. So, when our own faith shatters over the sharp edges of unrelenting pain and incurable sickness, faith itself is not destroyed for we are upheld even in our unfaith, by the arms of faith. This community of love and faith is the 'hospice' in which all are prepared for the 'way of the Lord'.

It is unlikely that many of us will die in our own bed, with the steady hand of a loved one to monitor the last heart beat. No matter. At the centre there is a body and a belief: the body is the body of Christ and the belief is a community of persons who will have the last look, the last touch and the last word. I do not need to speak in my own death, I am spoken for.

NOTES

1 *Death, Dying and Disposal*, edited by Gilbert Cope (London: SPCK, 1970).
2 In *Death and Dying – Current Issues in the Treatment of the Dying Person* (Cleveland: Case Western Reserve University Press, 1969), pp. 133–235.
3 For example, her books: *On Death and Dying* (New York: Macmillan, 1969); *Questions and Answers on Death and Dying* (New York: Macmillan, 1974); *Death, the Final Stage of Growth* (New York: Macmillan, 1975). See also: *The Human Encounter with Death*, by Stanislov Grof and Joan Halifax (New York: E. P. Dutton, 1978); *Dying, Death, and Grief: A Critically Annotated Bibliography and Source Book of Thanatology and Terminal Care*, by Michael Simpson (New York: Plenum Press, 1977); *Dying and Death: A Clinical Guide for Caregivers*, edited by D. Barton (Baltimore: Williams and Wilkins, 1977); *The Last Dance: Encountering Death and Dying*, by Lynne Ann DeSpelder and Albert Lee Strickland (Palo Alto, CA: Mayfield Publishing, 1982); *Living and Dying*, by Robert Lifton and Eric Olson (New York: Praeger, 1974).
4 This is the documented experience of Dr Michiko Nakajima, Director of Hospice Department, Mount of Olives Hospital, Naha, Japan. Reported in, 'Toward a Practical Theodicy: A Theological Interpretation of Pain and its Ministerial Application to Terminal Care with the Focal Interest in Cancer Pain Syndrome' by Michiko Nakajima, M.D., and Shuhei Nakajima, M.Div. Presented at Japan Evangelical Theological Society, Western Chapter Annual Conference, Kobe, Japan, 20 May 1985.
5 *The Hospice Movement: a Better Way of Caring for the Dying* (Briar Cliff Manor, NY: Stein and Day, 1978), p.3. For other sources on the hospice movement, see *A Hospice Handbook: A New Way of Caring for the Dying*, edited by Michael Hamilton and Helen Reid (Grand Rapids: Eerdmans, 1980). Both these books provide excellent bibliographies on hospice care.
6 *The Hospice Movement*, pp. 7ff.
7 'St Christopher's Hospice,' in *Death: Current Perspectives* (Palo Alto, CA: Mayfield Publishing, 1976), Edwin S. Shneidman, editor, pp. 516ff.
8 *The Hospice Movement*, p. 166.
9 Ibid., pp. 146, 147.
10 Ibid., p. 168.
11 Ibid., p. 169.
12 *Living With Death* (Grand Rapids, Eerdmans, 1983), p. 49.

13 Attributed to the Japanese doctor Senji Umehara, cited by Thielicke, ibid.
14 Ibid., pp. 52ff.
15 *Prayer and Modern Man* (New York: Seabury Press, 1979, pp. 71, 177. See also, Donald Bloesch, *The Struggle of Prayer* (New York: Harper and Row, 1980).
16 *Ethics*, p. 132. For Bonhoeffer's helpful discussion of the penultimate and the ultimate, see pp. 120ff.
17 Ibid., p. 126.

Select Bibliography

All quotations from the Bible refer to the Revised Standard Version, second edition (Division of Christian Education, National Council of Churches of Christ in the United States of America, 1971).

Aldwinckle, Russell. *Death in the Secular City*. Grand Rapids: Eerdmans, 1972.

Anderson, Ray S. *On Being Human – Essays in Theological Anthropology*. Grand Rapids: Eerdmans, 1982.

Bailey, Lloyd R., snr. *Biblical Perspectives on Death*. Philadelphia: Fortress Press, 1979.

Bailey, Robert W. *The Minister and Grief*. New York: Hawthorne, 1976.

Barth, Karl. *Church Dogmatics*, volume 3, part 2. Translated by Harold Knight *et al*. Edinburgh: T & T Clark, 1960.

Barton, David ed. *Dying and Death: A Clinical Guide for Caregivers*. Baltimore: Williams and Wilkins, 1977.

Becker, Ernest. *The Birth and Death of Meaning: An Interdisciplinary Perspective on the Problem of Man*, second edition. New York: Free Press, 1971.

Becker, Ernest. *The Denial of Death*. New York: Free Press, 1973.

Berkouwer, G.C. *Man: The Image of God*. Grand Rapids: Eerdmans, 1962.

Bloesch, Donald. *The Struggle of Prayer*. New York: Harper and Row, 1980.

Bonhoeffer, Dietrich. *Letters and Papers From Prison*. New York: Macmillan, New Enlarged edition, 1972.

Bonhoeffer, Dietrich. *True Patriotism – Letters, Lectures and Notes, 1939–45*. Edited and introduced by Edwin R. Robertson, translated by Edwin R. Robertson and John Bowden. London: Collins, 1973.

Bonhoeffer, Dietrich. *Ethics*. New York: Macmillan, 1955; London: Collins, 1963.

Bonhoeffer, Dietrich, *Creation and Fall*. London: SCM Press, 1959.

Bonhoeffer, Dietrich. *Act and Being*. London: Collins, 1962.

Brandon, S. G. F. *The Judgment of the Dead: The Idea of Life After Death in the Major Religions*. New York: Charles Scribner, 1967.

Bromiley, Geoffrey W., general editor. *The International Standard Bible Encyclopedia*, volume 1 (revised). Grand Rapids: Eerdmans, 1979. 'Death,' pp. 898–901.

Brown, Colin, general editor. *The New Interntional Dictionary of New Testament Theology*, volume 1. Grand Rapids: Zondervan, 1975. 'Death', 'Sleep', 'Dead', pp. 430–47.

Carlozzi, Carl G. *Death and Contemporary Man: The Crisis of Terminal Illness*. Grand Rapids: Eerdmans, 1968.

Carse, James P. *Death and Existence: A Conceptual History of Human Mortality*. New York: John Wiley, 1980.

Choron, Jacques. *Death and Western Thought*. New York: Collier Books, 1963.

Cope, Gilbert, ed. *Dying, Death and Disposal*. London: SPCK, 1970.

Crim, Keith, general editor. *The Interpreter's Dictionary of the Bible*. Supplementary Edition. Nashville: Abingdon Press, 1976. 'Death, Theology Of', pp. 219–22.

Davis, Stephen. 'Is Personal Identity Retained in the Resurrection?' In *Modern Theology*, forthcoming, 1986.

DeSpelder, Lynne Ann, and Strickland, Albert Lee. *The Last Dance: Encountering Death and Dying*. Palo Alto, CA: Mayfield Publishing, 1982.

Doss, Richard. *The Last Enemy*. New York: Harper and Row, 1974.

Eccles, John. *Facing Reality*. London: Heidelberg Science Library, 1970.

Eccles, John. *The Human Mystery*. Berlin/Heidelberg: Springer-Verlag, 1979.

Eliade, Mircea. *Death, Afterlife and Eschatology*. New York: Harper and Row, 1967.

Ellul, Jacques. *Prayer and the Modern Man*. New York: Seabury Press, 1979.

Erikson, Millard. *Christian Theology*, volume 2. Grand Rapids: Baker Book House, 1984.

Feifel, Herman, ed. *The Meaning of Death*. New York: McGraw-Hill, 1959.

Flew, Anthony, ed. *New Essays in Philosophical Theology*. London: SCM Press, 1955.

Froom, L. *The Conditionalist Faith of our Fathers*. Washington, DC: Review and Harald, 1966.

Fulton, Robert, ed. *Death and Identity*. New York: John Wiley, 1965.

Gatch, Milton McC. *Death: Meaning and Mortality in Christian*

Thought and Contemporary Culture. New York: Seabury Press, 1969.

Godin, André. *Death and Presence: The Psychology of Death and the Afterlife.* Brussels: Lumen Vitae Press, 1972.

Gordon, David Cole. *Overcoming the Fear of Death.* Baltimore: Penguin Books, 1972.

Gorer, Geoffrey. *Death, Grief and Mourning.* Garden City, NY: Doubleday, 1965.

Grof, Stanislav and Christina. *Beyond Death: The Gates of Consciousness.* New York: Thames and Hudson, 1980.

Grof, Stanislav, and Halifax, Joan. *The Human Encounter With Death.* New York: E. P. Dutton, 1978.

Grollman, Earl A. *Concerning Death: A Practical Guide for the Living.* Boston: Beacon Press, 1974.

Hafen, Brent Q., and Frandsen, Kathryn. *Faces of Death: Grief, Dying, Euthanasia, Suicide.* Englewood, CO: Morton Publishing, 1983.

Hamilton, Michael, and Reid, Helen, eds. *A Hospice Handbook: A New Way of Caring for the Dying,* Grand Rapids: Eerdmans, 1980.

Hardin, Garrett. *Promethean Ethics.* Seattle and London: University of Washington Press, 1980.

Heaney, John J. *The Sacred and the Psychic – Parapsychology and Christian Theology.* New York: Paulist Press, 1984.

Heidegger, Martin. *Being and Time.* Translated by John Macquarrie and Edward Robinson. New York: Harper and Row, 1962.

Hellwig, Monika. *What are they Saying About Death and Christian Hope?* New York: Paulist Press, 1978.

Hick, John. *Faith and Knowledge.* Ithaca, NY: Cornell University Press, 1957; second edition, 1966.

Hick, John. *Death and Eternal Life.* San Francisco: Harper and Row, 1976.

Hubbard, David Alan. *Why Do I Have to Die?* Glendale, CA: G/L Publications, 1978.

Humphreys, S.C., and King, Helen, ed. *Mortality and Immortality: The Anthropology and Archaeology of Death.* London: Academic Press, 1981.

Jackson, Charles O. ed. *Passing: The Vision of Death in America.* Westport, Conn. and London: Greenwood Press, 1977.

Jackson, Edgar. *Telling a Child About Death.* New York: Hawthorne, 1965.

Jüngel, Eberhard. *Death: The Riddle and the Mystery.* Translated by Ian and Ute Nicol. Philadelphia: Westminster Press, 1974.

Kalish, Richard A. ed. *Death, Dying, Transcending.* Farmdale, NY: Baywood Publishing, 1971.

Kalish, Richard A. ed. *Death and Dying – Views From Many Cultures.* Farmdale, NY: Baywood Publishing, 1979

Kastenbaum, Robert, and Aisenberg, Ruth. *The Psychology of Death.* Berlin: Springer-Verlag, 1972.

Kierkegaard, Søren. *Concluding Unscientific Postscript.* Translated by David F. Swenson and Walter Lowrie. Princeton, NJ: Princeton University Press, 1941.

Koestenbaum, Peter. *Is There an Answer to Death?* Englewood Cliffs, NJ: Prentice-Hall, 1976.

Kübler-Ross, Elizabeth. *Death, the Final Stage of Growth.* New York: Macmillan, 1975.

Kübler-Ross, Elizabeth. *Questions and Answers on Death and Dying.* New York: Macmillan, 1974.

Kübler-Ross, Elizabeth. *On Death and Dying.* New York: Macmillan, 1969.

Kushner, Harold S. *When Bad Things Happen to Good People.* New York: Avon Books, 1981.

Kuyper, Abraham. *The Death and Resurrection of Christ.* Grand Rapids: Zondervan, 1960.

Ladd, George E. *I Believe in the Resurrection of Jesus.* Grand Rapids: Eerdmans, 1975.

Lepp, Ignace. *Death and Its Mysteries.* Translated by Bernard Murchland. New York: Macmillan, 1968.

Lifton, Robert J. *The Broken Connection: On Death and the Continuity of Life.* New York: Simon and Schuster, 1979.

Lifton, Robert and Olson, Eric. *Living and Dying.* New York: Praeger, 1974.

Mackintosh, H.R. *Immortality and the Future.* London: Hodder and Stoughton, 1915.

McManners, John. *Death and the Enlightenment: Changing Attitudes to Death Among Christians and Unbelievers in Eighteenth Century France.* Oxford: Oxford University Press, 1981.

Macquarrie, John. *In Search of Humanity.* New York: The Crossroad Publishing, 1983.

Maeterlinck, Maurice. *Death.* New York: Arno Press, 1977.

May, William. 'The Sacral Power of Death in Contemporary Experience.' In *Perspectives on Death.* Liston O. Mills, ed. Nashville: Abingdon Press, 1979.

Metzger, Arnold. *Freedom and Death.* Translated by Ralph Manheim. London: Human Context Books, Chaucer Publishing, Ltd., 1973.

Mills, Liston O. ed. *Perspectives on Death.* Nashville: Abingdon Press, 1979.

Mitford, Jessica. *The American Way of Death.* New York: Simon and Schuster, 1963.

Moody, Dale. *The Word of Truth: A Summary of Christian Doctrine Based on Biblical Revelation*. Grand Rapids: Eerdmans, 1981.

Moody, Raymond. *Life After Death*. New York: Bantam Books, 1977.

Moody, Raymond. *Reflections on Life After Death*. New York: Bantam Books, 1978.

Morey, Robert A. *Death and the Afterlife*. Minneapolis: Bethany House, 1984.

Nakajima, Michiko and Shuhei. 'Toward a Practical Theodicy: A Theological Interpretation of Pain and its Ministerial Application to Terminal Care with the Focal Interest in Cancer Pain Syndrome.' Paper presented at Japan Evangelical Theological Society, Western Chapter Annual Conference, Kobe, Japan, May, 1985.

Neale, Robert E. *The Art of Dying*. New York: Harper and Row, 1973.

Nelson, J. Robert. *Human Life – A Biblical Perspective for Bioethics*. Philadelphia: Fortress Press, 1984.

Nowell, Robert. *What a Modern Catholic Believes About Death*. Chicago: Thomas Moore Press, 1972.

Ostrander, Sheila and Schroeder, Lynn. *Psychic Discoveries Behind the Iron Curtain*. Englewood Cliffs, NJ: Prentice-Hall, 1970.

Pannenberg, Wolfhart. *Jesus – God and Man*. London: SCM Press, 1968.

Pannenberg, Wolfhart. *Anthropology in Theological Perspective*. Translated by Matthew J. O'Connell. Philadelphia: Westminster Press, 1985.

Pattison, E. Mansel. 'The Experience of Dying', *American Journal of Psychotherapy*, 21, no. 1, 1967.

Pearson, Leonard. *Death and Dying – Current Issues in the Treatment of the Dying Person*. Cleveland and London: Case Western Reserve University Press, 1969.

Phillips, D.Z. *Death and Immortality*. Glasgow: The University Press, 1970.

Pieper, Josef. *Death and Immortality*. New York: Herder and Herder, 1969.

Prickett, John ed. *Death*. London: Lutterworth Educational, 1980.

Rahner, Karl. *On the Theology of Death*. Translated by C. H. Henkey. New York: Herder and Herder, revised edition, 1967.

Rahner, Karl. *Foundations of Christian Faith: An Introduction to the Idea of Christianity*. New York: Seabury Press, 1978.

Ramsey, Ian. 'Hell', in *Talk of God*, Royal Institute of Philosophy Lectures, volume 2. New York: St Martin's Press, 1969.

Rauschenbusch, Walter. *A Theology for the Social Gospel*. New York: Abingdon Press, 1917.

Rawlings, Maurice. *Beyond Death's Door*. New York: Thomas Nelson, 1981.

Richards, Lawrence O., and Johnson, Paul. *Death and the Caring Community*. Portland: Multnomah Press, 1980.

Robinson, Wheeler. *The Religious Ideas of the Old Testament*. London: Duckworth, 1913. 'Hebrew Psychology', pp. 79–83.

Russell, D. *The Method and Message of Jewish Apocalyptic*. London: SCM, 1964.

Rutherford, Richard. *The Death of a Christian: The Rite of Funerals*. New York: Pueblo Publishing, 1980.

Schmitt, Abraham. *Dialogue with Death*. Waco, Texas: Word Books, 1976.

Scott, Nathan A. jnr. *The Modern Vision of Death*. Richmond, VA: John Knox Press, 1967.

Sherry, Patrick. *Spirit, Saints, and Immortality*. Albany, NY: State University of New York Press, 1984.

Shibles, Warren. *Death: An Interdisciplinary Analysis*. Whitewater, WI: The Language Press, University of Wisconsin, 1974.

Shneidman, Edwin S., ed. *Death: Current Perspectives*. Palo Alto, CA: Mayfield Publishing, 1976.

Simpson, Michael. *The Facts of Death*. Englewood Cliffs, NJ: Prentice-Hall, 1979.

Simpson, Michael. *Dying, Death and Grief: A Critically Annotated Bibliography and Source Book of Thanatology and Terminal Care*. New York: Plenum Press, 1977.

Simpson, Michael, *The Theology of Death and Eternal Life*. Cork: Mercier Press, 1970.

Starenko, Ronald C. *God, Grass, and Grace: A Theology of Death*. St Louis, MO: Concordia Publishing, 1975.

Stoddard, Sandol. *The Hospice Movement: A Better Way of Caring for the Dying*. Briar Cliff Manor, NY: Stein and Day, 1978.

Sutcliffe, E. F. *The Old Testament and the Future Life*. London: Burns, Oates and Washburne, 1946.

Thielicke, Helmut. *Living With Death*. Translated by Geoffrey W. Bromiley. Grand Rapids: Eerdmans, 1983.

Thielicke, Helmut. *Being Human. . . Becoming Human*. Translated by Geoffrey W. Bromiley. Garden City, NY: Doubleday, 1984.

Tillich, Paul. *Systematic Theology*, volumes 2 and 3. Chicago: University of Chicago Press, 1957, 1963.

Tolstoi, L. *The Death of Ivan Ilych*. Translated by Louise and Aylmer Maude. New York: Health Sciences Publishing, 1973.

Torrance, Thomas F. *Theology in Reconstruction*. Grand Rapids: Eerdmans, 1965.

Torrance, Thomas F. *Space, Time and Resurrection*. Grand Rapids: Eerdmans, 1976.

Torrance, Thomas F. *Divine and Contingent Order*. Oxford: Oxford University Press, 1981.

Vaux, Kenneth. *Will to Live/Will to Die*. Minneapolis: Augsburg, 1978.

Walton, Douglas N. *On Defining Death: An Analytic Study of the Concept of Death in Philosophy and Medical Ethics*. Montreal: McGill-Queens University Press, 1979.

Weber, Otto. *Foundations of Dogmatics*, volume 1. Translated by Darrell Guder. Grand Rapids: Eerdmans, 1981.

Weisman, Avery D. 'Appropriate and Appropriated Death.' In *Death: Current Perspective*. Edwin S. Shneidman, ed. Palo Alto CA: Mayfield Publishing, 1976.

Westphal, Merold. *God, Guilt, and Death: An Existential Phenomenology of Religion*. Bloomington, Ind.: Indiana University Press, 1984.

Wingren, Gustaf. *Man and the Incarnation*. Edinburgh/London: Oliver and Boyd, 1959.

Wittgenstein, Ludwig. *Philosophical Investigations*. Oxford: Basil Blackwell, 1953.

Wolff, Hans Walter. *Anthropology of the Old Testament*. Translated by Margaret Kohl. Philadelphia: Fortress Press, 1974.

Wolff, Richard. *The Last Enemy*. Washington, DC: Canon Press, 1974.

Index

LaVergne, TN USA
25 February 2010
174314LV00001B/111/A